You Don't Know Crazy

My Life Before, During, After, Above and Beyond Mental Illness

Wambui Bahati

You Don't Know Crazy

Library of Congress Control Number: 2008941526

ISBN 978-0-9822398-0-3

Second Printing, Tradepaper Edition, January 2009

Cover Design by JLW World Press

Dedication

To my mother and father

Eva Athenia Davis Washington
and
John Louis Washington

Acknowledgments

I am grateful for everyone who helped make this book a reality. I thank all of you who believed in me when I couldn't, or (I suppose I should say) *wouldn't* believe in myself. I thank my spiritually beautiful daughters, Marie and Julie Blondina, for raising me to be the fine person that I am today. I thank them for their unwavering love, immeasurable support for this book and all of my projects, and their brilliant sense of humor.

I thank my mother and father, to whom this book is dedicated. I thank my sister Roberta, my brothers Joel and Justin, my aunt Thelma and my favorite ex-husband, Tony Blondina. I cannot tell my story without also telling part of their stories.

I thank my friend Kerry Nesbit for insightful feedback and countless hours of tedious editing of the original draft. I thank Bill and Grace Liberman, who provided a watchful eye and loving care for my children when I was not around to do so. I appreciate all of the kindness and support they have shown me and for letting me know they were there to help me in any way they could. I thank Cathie Holcombe for the endless support she has given me and my family and for not giving up on me when I gave her good cause to do so. I thank Tom Murray for not only being an extraordinary son-in-law, but for his kind, generous and immeasurable help and support for this book.

I thank Elaine Purple, Beth Melcher and The National Alliance on Mental Illness (Guilford County and North Carolina) for believing in the power of my story. I thank the numerous mental health associations, affiliates, clubhouses, treatment centers, conferences and conventions that not only showered me with love and hospitality; but also allowed me to share my story and encouraged me to get it on paper. I thank all my friends, acquaintances and others who never walked away or hung up the phone as I continuously (for nearly 10 years) talked about "the book . . . the book . . . the book."

A big shout out to Frances McNair, Deborah Shanks, The Greensboro Playwrights Forum, the Greensboro Dudley High School Class of '68, Mary Annecelli, Dr. Ridgely Abdul Mu'min, Eric Krebs, Jim Janek, Luis Montero, Tom Mallow, Sandra Carlson, Beverly Wideman, Lucy and Carroll Teeter, Vanessa Brown and Brenda and Hillary (from DC), Nancy, Janice Wise and dear Janet Werner.

Table of Contents

The following is a letter I received from a Social Security Administrative Law Judge in February 1993.

ISSUES

The issues in this case are whether the claimant is under a disability as defined by the Social Security Act and if so, when her disability commenced, the duration of the disability, and whether the insured status requirements of the Act are met for the purpose of entitlement to a period of disability and disability insurance benefits.

EVALUATION OF THE EVIDENCE

After a thorough evaluation of the entire record, it is concluded that the claimant has been disabled since July 12, 1991, and met the insured status requirements of the Social Security Act on that date and thereafter, through the date of this decision.

The claimant has a bipolar disorder and a personality disorder, which are considered to be "severe" under the Social Security Regulations.

The medical evidence of record reveals that the claimant has a diagnosed impairment due to a bipolar disorder, with a history of episodic periods manifested by the full symptomatic picture of both manic and depressive syndromes.

She also has a diagnosed impairment due to a personality disorder, characterized by inflexible and maladaptive personality traits which cause significant impairment in social and occupational functioning. This impairment is evidenced by intense and unstable interpersonal relationships and impulsive and damaging behavior.

The claimant has a long history of psychiatric hospitalizations and long term outpatient psychiatric treatment with counseling and medication. In spite of this treatment, the claimant continues to experience regular relapses.

Most recently, she was hospitalized for diagnoses of Bipolar Disorder II, Depression, and Personality Disorder. (Ex. 40) xxx xxxxx, M.D., performed a D.D.S. psychiatric evaluation on December 30, 1994, and diagnosed the claimant as having Bipolar cyclic (disorder) with a history of psychosis and a Borderline Personality Disorder. (Ex. 42)

Dr. xxxxx completed a Medical Assessment of Ability to Do Work-Related Activities (Mental) form, on which he indicated that the claimant had from very good to no ability to make occupational, performance, and personal-occupational adjustments, depending on illness and decompensation.

He noted that the claimant experienced frequent decompensation with at least 9 long term psychiatric admissions.

The claimant is disabled within the meaning of the Social Security Act and Regulations because she meets Listing 12.04.

* * *

I, the claimant, was successfully branded disabled and awarded disability insurance. Isn't that a strange term—awarded. It didn't feel like an award to me. I was compensated, drugged, and institutionalized and my life revolved around mental hospitals, therapy, court hearings, and the social security office. And I hated everything about all of it.

Introduction

It is estimated that more than 54 million Americans are diagnosed with a mental disorder in any given year. Of this number, more than two million are diagnosed with bipolar disorder, also known as manic-depressive illness.[1] I am familiar with this so-called disease. In 1993, at the age of 43, I received a medical diagnosis that officially placed me among the two million with bipolar disorder.

I know there are many who cannot speak openly about their mental health issues. Our society accepts many things these days—but mental illness still carries a stigma. I was able to speak openly because I didn't have a job, so I couldn't be fired. I didn't own any property where the neighbors could ostracize me. No one in my family was running for public office. I was sure that I had already been to

---

[1] Mental Health America, formerly known as the National Mental Health Association

hell and back, so I had nothing to lose by speaking about my experience with mental illness.

Wow! When I think of my life, as it was 15 or 20 years ago—when I think of the years when I was experiencing mental illness and how I was living and thinking then, it's as if I'm thinking of someone else. I'm no longer that same person. Who was that person?

* * *

If you are reading this book because you saw one of my performances, I thank you for coming to see me. It is an honor for me to tell my story—live and in person. Performing is one of my greatest joys. The desire to perform put me on the path to recovery. I remembered something that I loved to do and I found a way to do it.

As I travel around the United States telling my story, as I speak to mental health care consumers, their families and others, I am repeatedly asked two questions: 1) "What are some of the details of your story you're not telling because of time constraints?" and 2) "What did you do to turn your life around?" This book addresses both of these questions.

Because we are all different, not all of my answers may work for you or your loved ones. However, I can assure you that just looking for answers and taking control of your situation will change your life. I hope that I will, at the very least, persuade you to take charge and assume responsibility for your own life.

When I was at my lowest, I challenged myself to look at my lifestyle, mental attitude, and my will to live a good life. I'm here today in front of you in the words on this page to tell you that lifestyle changes restored my health.

I know that the specific steps I took may not be the specific steps you should take, but I am sure that positive, healthy lifestyle changes will help you (or anyone for that matter). Even if you still need traditional treatments, you will be far better off for asking questions, examining options, investigating alternative and natural therapies and taking control of your health.

I know there are people born with certain developmental issues and others who may have suffered a physical trauma that may not allow them to take full charge of their lives at this time. However, if you can read the words in this book and understand them, then I believe you can recover and heal your life—mind, body, soul and spirit. You have the power to 'rise above' (I did not say cure) any mental, physical or emotional challenges you have and have a joyful, peaceful and healthy life.

* * *

I know there may be some who are reading this and thinking *I hope she doesn't start with that 'love yourself, you have the power, you are magnificent, be grateful and get over it' crap.* Or you may be thinking, *'I hope she's not going to tell me how we all create our own reality and that I created my life and everything in it; therefore, I created this life situation and all my life pain that I hate.'*

I'm not going to *start* with any of that stuff. I'm going to start by sharing my story. I'm going to start by telling all of you that I was where some of you may be today. There was a time when I was angry and frustrated, depressed, and financially and spiritually broke. I remember the day I threw a book entitled *Faith In The Valley* by Iyanla Vanzant across my living room at the wall. I shouted to no one there, "I don't need any positive quotes and inspirational messages! I need some food. I need a decent place to live! I need some money!"

I'm going to share with you how I rewrote the script for my life. Part of it involved tearing out pages filled with drama—that for the longest time I thought was not only important, but also necessary. Sounds funny to get rid of drama in a script. Well, drama is great for the theater, however, in real life, drama is a drain, a drag, and stressful. Drama and being a "Drama Queen" are highly overrated.

I had to fire some of the actors in my life story and rewrite my script so that I was the star. I realized I could have more control over the scenes than I thought possible. I also realized that if I did not become the producer of my own life show, someone else would produce it for me. If I did not take charge of my script, I would continue to re-act instead of act. (No pun intended). I decided I would be the one who would have the final say about my life script. I eventually found out what part a positive quote and an inspirational message can play in rewriting one's life script.

My periods of mental instability were severe. They threatened my happiness, my family, and my life. My life was a disaster. I had doctors diagnosing me with all kinds of things. For a long time, I wasn't even sure I *wanted* my life. In fact, many times I was sure that I didn't, and I tried to end it.

However, at the last minute, someone would always save me from myself. Once, a doctor told me he didn't know how I could still be alive. He said, "When they brought you into the hospital, there was nothing we could do. I didn't do a thing." He told me to thank God. God was why I was alive.

I'll tell you the whole story later in the book, but I want to skip to the good part right now. I'm ok! And I have been for years. With a lot of work and reading and learning and trial and error, I pulled myself back from the brink. I am living proof that you can dig yourself out of an emotional hole and come back out into the light. It was sometimes challenging work, but it was worth it and I'm going to tell you how I did it, why I did it, and why it was worth it.

* * *

You might be wondering why I'm qualified to write a book about mental health issues. I will admit that I have been timid about sharing my story and discussing mental health because I'm not a doctor. However, as I have been reminded so often, I am a former patient. I know what it's like to be shackled and put in a sheriff's van and driven to a state mental hospital when I was not violent and my only crime was depression.

I know what it feels like when your own doctor and other caretakers will not even look at you when they speak to you, and how they can have a conversation about you while you are in the room as if you are not even there. Or, worse yet, assume that somehow my identity has merged with theirs. "How are *we* doing today?" "Did *we* sleep okay?" "Do you think *we're* about ready to go home?"

I know what it's like to hear mental health hospital staff say to each other—loud enough for patients to hear, "Why do they call 911 when they feel like killing themselves? Why don't they just die? Why do they call 911 and come here and get on our nerves?" I know what it's like to witness horrific scenes in a mental hospital and keep quiet because to tell someone would mean I would first have to admit that I was a mental patient and then of course it would be my word, a person with mental illness, against a *normal* hospital worker's word.

I know what it feels like to be admitted into a hospital, shown to my room and told to unpack only to have someone from hospital administration say, "You're going to have to leave. We just checked, and your insurance is not accepted at this hospital."

I know what it's like to have to take four medications for behavioral and emotional problems, and eight medications to control the emotional and physical side effects caused by the first four medications. I know what it feels like to take a whole bottle of antidepressants with a bottle of scotch on a sunny day in October and wake up in the psychiatric ward of DC General Hospital. I know what it feels like to not eat or sleep for five days in a row. I also know what it's like to sleep for five days straight.

I know what it feels like to cry uncontrollably for no visible reason. I know what it's like to keep telling my story over and over and over again to a new therapist because the staff at my outpatient clinic keeps changing. I know what it feels like to make a key chain during in-patient arts and crafts and feel so proud because I cut out the flower and glued it to a block of wood all by myself.

I remember that day. I was in a state hospital in North Carolina. These two young college women had come in to have art therapy with us. I assumed they had come because of some college requirement. I had never seen them before.

I liked them because they were friendly, their voices were soothing and they looked at us and listened to what we had to say as if it really mattered. One of them asked, "Is anyone interested in making a key chain?" I was like a five year old.

"I would like to make a key chain."

I sat down at a table that was covered with colorful pages from magazines, a few bottles of Elmer's glue and a few pairs of tiny round-tipped scissors like the children use in kindergarten. I found a page with a pink flower that intrigued me. When I was on a lot of medication, it was sometimes hard to keep my hands from shaking. So, this was going to be a bit of a challenge.

I slowly and carefully cut around the petals of that flower. I felt hypnotized by the flower and edging the scissors around ever so gently so as not to snip a petal too closely. I barely allowed myself to breathe. I wanted it to be perfect.

"Very nice." One of the college students said when she saw my flower all cut out. "Would you like to glue it to this piece of wood now?"

I was ready for that task too. I concentrated. The idea was to use just the right amount of glue. Too much and the whole thing would look tacky and be ruined. I held my breath. Positioning the flower just right was very important. I had to work quickly. I didn't want the glue to dry before I had it in just the right position.

When I was finished gluing, one of the students put a tiny chain through the hole in the wood and fastened it. She held it up so that the others could see. "What about this one? This is also a very beautiful key chain." If I were ever to win an Academy Award, I cannot imagine feeling any prouder.

I lived through mental illness and now I tell my story to patients and professionals around the country. I am qualified to talk about mental illness because I lived it. I believe my opinion counts and yours does too.

* * *

I do not take mental health lightly, and in no way do I discount the many honorable mental health professionals out there, or anyone who may be dealing with mental health issues at this time. I just want to expand the conversation to include everyone and to include all parts of us—our whole bodies, our minds, and our spirits.

Each of us has been born with the challenge of remaining balanced and sane in an insane and unbalanced world. We live in a world of wars, hunger, inequitable laws, unenforceable laws, laws written on our behalf that we cannot interpret without paying for a lawyer's help, an artificial calendar and manufactured time, devitalized food, impure water, prejudice, fear and anger. Wow! How does anyone remain sane, whole, happy and disease-free?

I'm not going to focus on the stigma of mental health, or why we don't have better mental health coverage, or whether or not psychiatry is art or science. I know that as I'm writing this book, laws and systems are being put in place to deny us, or block us from having a say in the type of mental health treatments we receive. This makes it even more important for each of us to understand who we are, what we are capable of, and how innately powerful we are.

I want to focus on what we can do for ourselves. I want to focus on our individual talents and strengths and all that we have control over. Remember: do not get caught up in worrying about what is wrong with your life, the system, or the world. Focus on what *is* right in your life and the one thing that you can control—YOURSELF.

* * *

I have wanted to write this book for a long time. At first I wasn't sure if I could do it—that is tell my story—and tell the truth. I know I'm totally exposing myself. This book is an example of being totally honest with you and myself—totally open and vulnerable. I was afraid of what the doctors might say, what the pharmaceutical companies might say, what my ex-husbands might say, what my neighbors might say and what you might say. Well, I grew past that.

Now, here is my story:

PART ONE - My Story

It's a bit like a musical I was in, *The Wiz*, which is an African American stage version of *The Wizard of Oz*. Like Dorothy, the lead character, I had to travel a long road and face many challenges before I learned enough to appreciate my life and how to not just survive, but live. And like Dorothy, the greatest lesson I would learn is that I too had the silver slippers (in *The Wiz* they were silver), the power—the whole time, and did not realize it. I was busy searching for answers everywhere except within me.

Life started out good for me. I had a mama, a daddy, two brothers, and a sister. My sister Roberta was the oldest. I made my entrance two years after Roberta. My mother says, before I was born, she thought she could predict whether I was going to be a boy or a girl. She predicted I would be a boy. She also thought I would be her last child. Therefore, she decided to name me after my father. I was to be John Louis Washington, Jr.

After my birth at 7:51 on the morning of January 26th 1950, it was confirmed that I was a girl. However, my mother decided to just go ahead and name me John Washington anyway. She did change my middle name to Ann. My official birth records said, 'Child's Name: John Ann Washington.'

My brother Joel followed two years after me. My brother Justin arrived five years after Joel. We lived in a small, two-bedroom house in Greensboro, North Carolina. Greensboro is in the northeastern part of the state of North Carolina, close to the Virginia border and a few hours south of Washington, DC.

The year I was born, 1950, the price of a new car was around $1,750 and the average price of a new house was about $14,500. A loaf of bread was

14¢ and milk was 82¢ a gallon. A first class stamp was 3¢ and the minimum wage was 75¢ per hour.

This is also the year the president of the United States, Harry S. Truman, ordered the construction of the hydrogen bomb. Television was still a relatively new invention. A new table model would have cost about $200, which was a lot of money for my family. My family would not own a TV until a few years later. We also did not own a car at this time.

I have only two memories of my life between birth and first grade—and even first grade is sketchy. I remember going with my family to visit one of my father's relatives in South Carolina and singing a song for whomever the woman was we visited.

The other memory is of me at Sunday school. I don't know what happened, but I started to cry and I couldn't stop. I wanted my mama. The Sunday school teacher tried to calm me down and after she realized that was not going to happen, she left the room and came back with my mama.

I wanted my mother to hug me, but instead she took me outside and said she would spank me if I did not stop crying. I managed to stop crying before she found a twig.

During my elementary grades, I have some uncomfortable memories of standing by a picture window in our living room waiting for my mama to come home from her "day work," cleaning up white people's houses. I could see the bus stop from that window.

She'd get off the bus with a bag of groceries in one arm and a pocketbook thrown over the other. I was always happy to see her come home.

If you had to sum my mother up in one word, the word would be proud. Yes, she was self-righteous and self-important. This was my mother's answer to surviving life's uncertain journey. I thought my mother was beautiful and when I was young, I wanted to be like her.

I didn't mind my mother doing the cleaning part of her jobs, but I hated that she took care of those white children too. After all, she was my mother and I wanted her to only take care of us—me, my sister Roberta, and my two younger brothers, Joel and Justin.

I don't have many memories of Justin and Joel when we were young children. I do remember having fun with them riding our bikes, skating and playing one-two-three red light. Nevertheless, I was mostly into what was referred to, as 'girl stuff' like dolls, sewing and making mud pies outside. They were into marbles, cowboys, go-carts and miniature army men.

Roberta amazed me with her ability to focus on a television show, concentrate on an algebra problem, draw, and carry on a funny conversation with me—all at the same time. Roberta and I got good grades in school. However, for her, it came easier.

I never liked having a lot of rules to follow. Therefore, for that reason school was not particularly enjoyable to me. However, knowing there were no options, I decided to make the best of it.

Joel was smart and clever but didn't get the grades in school that Roberta and I got. My mother and his teachers held this against him. He was often punished when he got a low grade in a subject. To this day, I do not understand why people will not accept that we are all different and have different talents. We all process information in different ways. Why are we so eager to fit everyone in the same box?

When Joel was about 10 or 11, he had a newspaper route. On Friday evenings, I would go with him to deliver the papers and help collect the money from the customers. I felt so happy and carefree on those evenings. We laughed a lot at how poor my newspaper throwing skills were. I was proud and happy that he was making money.

Justin was about eight years younger than I was. Most of my memories of him are of a baby. I don't remember who took care of Justin while my mama was working. A few times, I stayed home from school to watch him. In general, I mostly have memories of my brothers always being in trouble with my mother for not doing their homework, breaking something in the house, or being caught in some lie about their homework or breaking something in the house.

Both of my parents worked hard, taught us right from wrong, and did what they could to instill a sense of dignity in us. Although we were not a huggy, kissy family, there was plenty of love in our home.

Church was important to my family and me when I was growing up. Next to school, church was my biggest social outlet. People in my community did two main things. They went to work and they went to church. When my friends and I met someone new, it wasn't a question of, "Do you go to church?" The question was, "What church do you go to?"

There was an element of surprise or even disdain for anyone who might answer, "I don't go to church." That was not an acceptable answer. How could anyone not know or believe that Jesus died for their sins?

Many of my school friends also went to my church. By the time I was ten, I liked Sunday school and church. I believed in Jesus. I believed in God. I believed in the church. I believed in religion. I believed in the Bible. I believed in the Bible stories. I believed because I was afraid not to believe.

From my Bible lessons, I understood that God could be angered easily and he was into revenge. I believed God was a powerful spirit that looked like a giant man with a long beard. I assumed he hung out somewhere above the clouds. I was too afraid to ask questions about church because I was afraid God might get angry with me. Therefore, I didn't want to take any chances on upsetting God by asking the wrong questions.

One of the things that puzzled me the most is how, on the one hand, I heard God was loving and forgiving, but on the other hand, if you angered him, he could punish you by sending you to a fiery hell where you would burn for the rest of eternity.

I didn't understand how this powerful, all-knowing, all-seeing being could allow bad things to happen. How could he allow little babies to die? How could he allow somebody's parents to die? How could he allow someone's house to burn down?

Some of my friends told me the only music they were allowed to listen to on Sundays was gospel or religious music, and they were not allowed to dance on Sundays. My mother allowed us to listen to regular radio music and even dance on Sundays if we wanted to. However, I wasn't sure I wanted to have fun on Sunday.

I didn't know if that was one of the things that God liked or not. I was never sure exactly what God's rules were. I knew about the Ten Commandments, but outside of that, different individuals seemed to have their own unwritten rules about what was a sin and what wasn't. I found this confusing and frustrating. Eventually, I just went with the flow. I didn't ask questions about any of this because I didn't want to make God—or other people—upset with me.

People got dressed up to go to my church. For some of us, church was the only reason to buy pretty and fancy clothes. I don't know if it was or not, but I got the impression that for a woman to show up at church without a hat was a sin. At our church, the women wore stunning, colorful hats with veils or lace or flowers or bows or sequins or beads or all of the above.

We would start getting ready for church on the Saturday night before. My father hardly ever went to church with us. I assumed it was because he worked the late shift at the post office. He didn't get off work until midnight and then had to be back again by three in the afternoon. In our house, each of us would decide on what we would wear to church the next day.

My mother would make sure my sister, brothers and I took a bath. She would straighten Roberta's and my hair with the hot comb. On some occasions, she would set our hair with rollers so that we would have curls for church. Usually, for school, we just had braids or a ponytail. I always looked forward to the times when I got to have curly hair.

For a while, Roberta and I wore identical outfits to church. The only difference would be the color and size. Perhaps Roberta's would be baby blue and mine would be pink or vice versa. I liked that. Roberta didn't think it was cool to be dressing exactly like her younger sister. So, that didn't last very long.

The women wore various colored gloves to match their outfits. Before we were teenagers, my sister and I wore white gloves, shiny black patent leather shoes and crinoline slips underneath our dresses. My mother would starch the crinoline slips until they literally stood up by themselves. When we put our dresses over the slips, our dresses would stand out far from our bodies. I felt like a princess.

My favorite holidays were Christmas and Easter and I always looked forward to the programs that the church would have. By the time I was in Junior High School, I even looked forward to participating in them. I loved the Christmas story about Jesus' birth and I used to imagine how Mary and Joseph must have felt when they were turned away from the inn. By the time I was in high school, I was really interested in how the immaculate conception occurred. But, I didn't dare ask.

I don't remember how old I was when I found out Santa Claus was a fantasy. I was really angry with my parents and every other adult who'd led me to believe Santa actually stopped by my house while I was sleeping and delivered my presents—and who thought it was cute that I should sit on some fat, hairy man's lap and tell my deepest desires to him. I never fully trusted adults after that. I figured if they could have every child believing this, they had the ability to make us believe anything they wanted us to—true or not.

I have pleasant memories of church. And although there were many aspects that I didn't understand and even found frightening, I did find comfort in believing that Jesus and God would protect me—if I didn't sin. I was always trying to toe the line—trying to be the good Christian—trying to be a good child of God.

Oh there was that one thing—segregation. Segregation interfered with my joy and threatened to end my dreams and diminished my self-esteem. Segregation—and the Jim Crow laws, forced me to ride in the back of the bus and go through the side door of the one movie theater that would let me in, and always reminded me that I was a second-class citizen.

I was about six the day I became fully aware of racial differences. Up until that time, I just accepted everything around me as normal. But on this particular day, I was downtown with my mother. It was summer and awfully hot. I don't remember what store we were in, but I recall the fanciest water fountain I'd ever seen. In fact, I don't think that I even knew it was a water fountain until I saw other people drinking from it.

Most water fountains that I had encountered looked more or less like a toilet. But this one was different. It was taller and shiny. I was on my tip toes and the water was just touching my lips when I felt my mother grab my arm and yank me away from the fountain. She hurt my arm and I was totally confused. What had I done wrong? My mother yelled at me, "Didn't you see the sign?" I thought my mother had lost her mind. *What is wrong with her? What is she talking about? Why is she yelling at me?*

"You see this sign?" My mother pointed to a sign about a foot above the water cooler. "It says 'White Only'. This is not for you. If it doesn't say 'Colored', it's not for you!" I got it. I understood. If it doesn't say Colored, it's not for me. My mother pulled me out of the store. She was much calmer after we left the store. In fact, her whole attitude changed. She bought me a doughnut and we went home and never spoke of that incident again.

Even as a child, I started to understand that my mother had to put on a show in that store. My mother didn't care that I had drank from that water fountain. It would be a few years later before I realized how necessary it was for her to act the part of the 'outraged Colored mother'. She needed to play that part so that all of the outraged white people looking at me and her would not have to play the part of 'outraged white people' that day. They could relax knowing that this Colored mother had put her Colored child in her place and they wouldn't have to do it.

My mother was not only an extremely proud woman; she was, at times, a very defiant woman. She didn't take no 'mess' from any one—especially white people. My mother taught us not to talk back and she kept us in line, but she was quick to put people in their place herself if she felt she was being disrespected.

On one occasion, before my mother started working as a nurse's aide and was still cleaning up different white people's houses, my mother went to work for a new family. My mother says that she was not allowed to use the vacuum cleaner and the lady didn't even have a dust pan. She said the lady would come around every half hour asking, "What have you done today, Eva?"

When it was time to go home, it was customary for the domestic help to sit in the back seat of the car. My mother got in the front seat next to the woman. The woman, all flustered, said, "Now, Eva, you gon' have to get in the back seat." My mother said "No, I don't have to get in the back seat. I'm gon' ride up here with you from now own." And Mama didn't budge from that seat. When the woman dropped my mother off at the bus stop she said, "I'll pick you up at the same time tomorrow morning. We have a lot of work to do." My mother said, "You won't pick me up because I won't be here."

"When will I see you again Eva?"

"Never!"

And my mother never went back to that lady. My mother in later years would say, "Rosa Parks was not the first Colored woman to ever refuse to give up her seat. It just happened that it made the news that day when she did it."

My mother eventually had two favorite families that she liked working for. They were the Gerald family and Dr. Lusk and his family. Both of these families had children. Sometimes I feel like these white children are my brothers and sisters. They just lived in a bigger, fancier house and had more money. But didn't we share the same mother?

They ate food that my mother cooked for them just like she cooked it for us. She wiped their noses and she wiped ours. She would bring home books that they had read and didn't want anymore and we would read them. So, we read the same things and even wore some of the same clothes sometimes. They were the white brothers and sisters I never knew whose lives were influenced in some part by my mother.

I knew that racially, things were not fair. I didn't understand why we were considered not as good as—or not as worthy as white people. I learned that there were people who hated me, hated my mother, and hated my father and friends just because we had brown skin.

They didn't want us in their schools and playgrounds and didn't want to sit next to us in the movies. There were those who treated us with less respect than they would treat a stray dog. I couldn't think about it. I filed these feelings and these thoughts away somewhere. I don't know where. I didn't care at the time. I just couldn't think about these things and get up in the morning and go to school and have fun.

I suppose the most painful time was when I would watch white children play on a certain swing set or some other interesting piece of play equipment in a park. It looked like they were having fun and I wanted to try it too. But I knew I was not allowed to play on it or go in that playground. I tried not to think about the situation. To do so would be too painful and I felt there wasn't anything we could do about it. It was the way things were and I—we all just lived with it.

Daddy. Ah! My daddy was a genius. At least I thought he was. He was so smart about everything. He read a lot. In fact, after his death, I found out his book collection contained many of the books that I discovered during my journey to reclaim my life. Many of the books we found in his room were time-less self-help and spiritually enlightening books. He was also a writer.

Justin saved several published books that had my daddy's poems and song lyrics in them. He was quite the romantic. Here are two poems I found in a book published in 1945 entitled *Songwriters and Poets of America*:

WHEN THE BELLS OF FREEDOM RING
Oh! How glad we will be
When the world is all free
And our boys return home
Never again to roam.
When the bells of freedom ring
Our boys will come marching home
Never again to roam;
When the bells of freedom ring
Empty arms will then fill
And lonely hearts will thrill;

Joyful songs we will sing–
When, the bells of freedom ring!

UNDER A SKY OF BLUE
When the gray skies turn to blue
And I'm cuddling close to you,
Sharing love without measure–
That is my greatest pleasure;
Under a sky of blue,
Just you and I;
Under a sky of blue,
With love that'll never die.
This is really sublime–
Although I haven't a dime.
Under a sky of blue,
We are riding high.
If this isn't romance,
Then I haven't a chance.
But I'm well pleased,
Lying here in the breeze–
Under a sky of blue
With lovely you.

My father's bio in the back of the book reads:

John L. Washington is serving with the U.S. Army. He has been writing for four years and has had his work published in another national poetry anthology. He is the author of one published song and has lyrics for 20 others ready for the consideration of music publishers. Address: Co, I 368 inf., APO 93, San Francisco, California.

When I was about 11 or 12, I remember seeing a 78 rpm record down in our basement with my father's name on the label right beside where it said "lyrics by." As I sit here writing this, my eyes fill with tears because I miss my father so. And because I now realize how much I am like my father. He used to spend hours in his room playing with the latest technical gadgets. I do that same thing today. In the 70s, my daddy owned one of the first Radio Shack personal computers when hardly anyone knew what a personal computer was.

There weren't a lot of computer programs back then. My father created a program that would create and print mailing lists. The ability to print mailing lists in your own home was unheard of at that time. Some of the neighbors would ask him to print their Christmas card lists. If he were still alive, he would be as fascinated as I am with the advances that have been made in computer and digital technology. I would love to show him the new iPhone.

My father could fix anything electrical. People would drop off their old broken radios and televisions at our house and my father would fix them up just like new. He studied engineering for a short while at the Greensboro's North Carolina Agricultural and Technical College, which is now known as A&T State University. However, he had to leave school for financial reasons after I was born. He always talked about having his own business. My mother wanted him to have a good job with benefits, save his money, and support his family—and pay his bills on time.

I wish I'd known him better. My father had an enormous sense of humor and could be very funny. I don't know where he came up with some of the jokes he used to tell. He could do 10 minutes of funny stories just about things on the Camels cigarette pack.

Yes, my father was a Camels man. No filters for him. I hardly ever recall seeing my father without a cigarette in his hand. While he was a man who could tell us funny stories and make everybody fall on the floor laughing, there were moments when he was extremely sad. He didn't talk much at those times.

As a child, I knew he had pain—emotional pain. But as a child, I did not understand emotional pain. So, I did not understand why he needed to drink alcohol. I didn't understand why he needed to drink so much alcohol that he could sometimes miss paying the light bill or other bills—or all the bills. I didn't understand that then.

I didn't understand then, and even now I can't fully appreciate how it must have felt to be a black man in the segregated South. How must it have felt to be an intelligent, hard-working man who served his country in the Army but who, like the rest of us, could not walk through the front door or use the bathroom in most establishments?

I can't imagine how it must feel, when you're struggling to make ends meet, to have your wife go to work for wealthy white people and hear her talking about the new car or the new washing machine that the man she works for bought for his family. Or, to hear your wife say, "I'm going to have to work late tonight because the family I work for is having a really fancy dinner party." And know that your children are excited about this because it means she'll bring home whatever fancy food is left over.

My happiest memories with my father are listening to Louis Prima and Pearl Bailey albums and watching The Ed Sullivan Show on Sunday evenings. It was a big event when we knew somebody 'Colored' was going to be on television. I remember receiving a Sunday night phone call and before the person on the other end would even say their name, they'd say, "There's some Colored people on TV."

I never mourned my father's death. At the time of his death he was in such pain. He died from lung cancer and complications of alcoholism. At the time of his death I was struggling with my own emotional and financial pain. I'm grateful that my two daughters got to meet him and know him as well as they could, and vice versa. When we found out he was terminally ill, I was in my late 30s, and by then had dealt with my own emotional pain long enough to realize that all these years my father had medicated himself with alcohol to relieve *his* emotional pain.

My father's friends and our neighbors used to call him "say-nothing-Wash" because, in general, he was very quiet and a loner. He would speak to you if you spoke to him and he was friendly. However, he didn't talk much and seemed uncomfortable around people unless he'd been drinking or wanted to impress one of us kids with one of his standup comedy routines.

One day, when I was in the fifth grade, after we came home from school, my sister had to call my mama at work, who called the doctor, who called the police. Two policemen came to our house and stood outside my father's bedroom door. It seems my sister had heard what sounded like a gun shot, and she couldn't get my father to open the door.

The policemen said they wouldn't hurt him and they didn't. One policeman said to him, "Mr. Washington, just give us the gun." Eventually, my father opened the door and gave the officer the gun. I saw the officer give my daddy some money. And, that was the end of that. Eventually, my father patched up the bullet hole. We never spoke of the incident again until I added a short scene about it in my show *Balancing Act - The Musical.*

When my father died, on February 17, 1989, I was actually happy that he was no longer in pain. The U.S. Department of Veterans Affairs (V.A.) issued my father/our family a burial flag on the occasion of his death in commemoration of his service to his country. Yet, at the time of his death, my father was still not a free man in his own country. And, when my father died, I wished that I could go with him because I wanted to alleviate my pain too. I was 39 at the time of his death and was constantly in and out of psychiatric hospitals.

Despite my father's drinking and segregation, my childhood was, for the most part, fun and good.

We didn't have any cousins or extended family in Greensboro. I looked forward to taking trips to Goldsboro where my mother was born. We would stay with my grandparents and my Aunt Thelma and visit a never-ending list of other relatives and family friends.

Grandma Beady's parents had been born slaves. By the time she was born, slavery had ended and her parents were sharecroppers or tenant farmers who gave a part of each crop back as rent. Beady married Walter Davis. Beady and Walter had two daughters. Their first born was named Thelma and the second and last child was named Eva. Eva is my mother. Grandma Beady was tall and rail-thin. She had high cheekbones, smooth skin and was gorgeous.

One of my most special memories was watching Grandma Beady, Aunt Thelma and my mother getting dressed for church. They were dignified, strong, beautiful, stubborn, and incredibly stylish. They made their own clothes, styled their own hair and wore red lipstick. To this day, I buy and wear only red lipstick. To me lipstick is not lipstick if it's not red.

They smelled good too. They would gently spray me and my sister Roberta with cologne before leaving for church. For the longest time, I thought the name for perfume and cologne was "to a wild rose." It turns out that was just the name of the Avon cologne that my mother always bought. Before church or any other special occasion she would ask, "Do you want a little 'to a wild rose'?" So, I thought anything that sprayed and smelled good was called "to a wild rose."

Me and my next door neighbor in Greensboro, Deborah, would sometimes play a game where we would put powdered Nestle Chocolate down in our gums and pretend we were dipping snuff like my grandma Beady and Aunt Thelma did. Snuff was a powdered tobacco that was held in the mouth, usually in the lower lip, rather than smoked. The person would have to spit at intervals in order not to swallow the tobacco. I don't remember Beady smiling a lot. She could be moody and was often angry with my grandfather. To this day I don't know why she was so angry with him.

My grandfather was round compared to my grandmother. He had jet black skin. He was extremely intelligent about world politics and mechanical things. I don't know how he knew what he knew. He would come home from his job covered with thick black grease. I think he fixed tractors and other heavy-duty machines. When he walked through the back door, I remember grandma Beady angrily saying to him, "Don't sit down on my furniture until you change your clothes and don't touch anything." He was quiet, but once you got him talking he could talk on and on. He seemed to know everybody and their "kin folks" for miles around.

We all loved going to our grandma's. She didn't give us a lot of chores to do. In the evenings, she would give my Aunt Thelma money and tell her to take us to Williams Street to Wayne Dairy to get ice cream. My favorite was butter pecan. On about our second day there, she'd give Aunt Thelma money to take us downtown to Kresses dime store or Woolworth's to get us a toy of our choice so we would have something to entertain ourselves with during our stay.

I would usually choose a ric rac—the paddle with the ball attached by a long elastic or a set of ball and jacks. A slick linoleum covered the long hallway that literally went straight from the front door to the back door of the house. The linoleum was great for throwing and picking up jacks because it was so smooth. We'd also get a shopping trip to a fabric store. Roberta and I would get to pick out a few pieces of fabric to take home for my Aunt Thelma to make us shorts and play clothes for the summer, or dresses for the coming school year or church.

My Grandma Beady fed us. I can taste the fresh corn on the cob and black-eyed peas and chicken fried up in lard. When she wanted a chicken for dinner, she would just walk right out into her back yard and chose one of the many that were there. She would wring that chicken's neck like it was a rag doll. Then she'd put it in a big pot of hot water and pick the feathers off. I didn't like eating those chickens. I wanted store bought chicken. She had a huge garden with all kinds of vegetables and a pecan tree.

Just as it got dark, we'd go out to catch lightening bugs. Sometimes we'd use our bare hands and then other times we'd catch them with a jar and a lid. My brother Joel would put holes in his jar lids so, according to him, the lighting bugs could breathe and stay alive longer.

In the living room was Grandma's rocker chair. It sat across the room from the TV. The TV was on a low table underneath the front window. This allowed her to have the best of both worlds. She could watch the news and her soap operas and never miss anything that was happening on Greenleaf Street.

When Grandma was not in the living room, my sister, brothers and I had a lot of fun sitting, relaxing and climbing all over that chair. However, the minute we heard her coming we would immediately move to another seat. That was Grandma's chair and we never forgot that. She kept bags of candy underneath that chair. We also knew not to touch that candy. I'm sure we found that out the hard way. I'm sure one of us thought it would be a good idea to help ourselves to that candy at some time or another. And, I'm sure she let us know in no uncertain terms that it wasn't a good idea.

In the evenings, she'd take out a cigar box with her comb and hair rollers from underneath that same chair. She'd carefully part her soft graying hair into small sections and wind each section on a small hair roller. Her fingers worked like magic. She didn't even need a mirror. We'd all sit looking at her anticipating the question we loved to hear. She'd finish her hair and put the cigar box back underneath the chair; she'd pull out a bag of candy and ask, "Do y'all want some candy?" Yes we wanted some candy!

My grandma had the most luxuriously soft bed. She made the bedspread and quilts by hand. The bedspread was white and fluffy. I liked looking at the quilts that she and my aunt made. I'd make a game of picking out the fabric patches that were the same as my clothes made from the same fabric. I would melt in that bed. Sleep came so easily there. However, like her chair, I was reminded that it was not my bed and would quickly be transported to the room where me and my sister and brothers slept.

My grandparents and Aunt Thelma had a dog named Spot. I never cared much for Spot. I would never have hurt him or anything. I just was not interested in Spot—or any dog for that matter. So, I kept out of his way and he kept out of mine. Interestingly enough, to this very day, some fifty years later, I feel the exact same way about dogs. Keep them out of my way and I'll stay out of theirs.

My Grandma's house was right across the street from Scott's Barbecue. The barbecue was so-o-o good. Almost as good as Beady's homemade pork crackling. It wasn't until I was an adult that I found out Scott's Barbecue had tables inside and that Mr. Scott was a black man. We always got our barbecue from the small takeout window outside of the store because black people where not allowed to eat inside.

As summer would come to an end, either my grandfather would drive us, or we would take the train back to Greensboro. I also have happy memories of the last hot days before fall arrived in Greensboro, ice cream trucks, and chilidogs at the local Woolworth's. Though it was a shame we couldn't sit and eat our chilidogs like white people did. The Woolworth's lunch counter was a "whites" only counter.

The year was about 1963. I was about 13.

Roberta would come home from high school all fired up about something some guy at the Agricultural and Technical College had said.

"I think he's fine." She'd smile and give a heavenly sigh each time she'd say how fine he was. (In the sixties that meant he was cute).

"Is he your boyfriend?" I asked.

"No. He's not my boyfriend, but I do think he's fine—and he's smart too." She'd go on to say, "He said we are just as good as white people. We should be able to go in the front door of the Carolina Theater just like anybody else—and sit down at Woolworth's and eat our food like the white people do."

"Yea. Well what is this 'fine college boy' going to do about it?"

"We're going to march."

"What?"

"Jesse said . . ."

"Is that your boyfriend's name?"

"He's not my boyfriend. His name is Jesse Jackson. And Jesse said we have to let white people know that we are people too and are entitled to the same rights that the white people have."

Eventually, my sister and her friend Cassandra convinced my mother to let us go downtown to the demonstrations. My mother was frightened for us. And with good reason. There were too many stories of young and old being killed or permanently disabled due to being attacked by dogs, the force of water from a fire hose, or brutally beaten by white people who were determined to keep black people "in their place."

One afternoon my sister told me to let her know when Cassandra arrived. I stood looking out of the picture window.

"She's here Roberta!" I yelled to my sister when I saw Cassandra drive up.

However, it was my mama who burst into the living room from the kitchen. She looked at me and then she turned to Cassandra who was still standing by the front door. My mother had her arms folded and was unconsciously scratching her elbow, something she did when she was nervous or upset.

"I don't know why y'all want to get in this mess. Can't we just leave well enough alone? You know there was a time when we were slaves. We couldn't own or do anything. Y'all have it good today."

My sister, who had entered the room, chimed in, "Mama we are still only second class citizens. Mama, they make us go in the side door of the Carolina Theater . . ."

"There was a time when we couldn't go in at all," my mother snapped back. "Let's just leave everything like it is. We're doing okay now. It's not perfect, but it's better than it was when I was coming up."

Roberta asked, "Mama, are white people better than we are?"

My mother was silent for a while. The she stood up and headed back toward the kitchen. Mama didn't look back. She just talked as she walked into the kitchen. "I want you back in this house by 8:30. No later. Please! Please stick together! And, watch what you say and who you say it to. Everybody that's a Negro ain't necessarily your friend. Did y'all hear what I said?"

"Yes." We answered in unison.

I went with Cassandra and my sister. We went to the church where we met up with others and prepared for the march. There was a brief prayer service and we received instructions. We marched two by two in silence. Looking straight ahead. Not responding to racial slurs, shoves or even being spat on. We marched two by two. As we walked down Elm Street, I could see angry white people and fire trucks in my peripheral vision. I don't know why I wasn't afraid.

The police started arresting people. I don't know why I wasn't afraid. We returned the next night. Each night more and more people were arrested. And each night that followed, it seemed like more people showed up to take the place of those who had been arrested the night before. And there were more arrests. And more people showed up to take the places of those people. And we kept coming.

Before long, the jails were full of demonstrators who had been arrested. The Greensboro Coliseum was full of demonstrators who had been arrested. A National Guard Armory building was full of demonstrators who had been arrested.

Eventually, the time came when the police would give us a choice as to whether or not we wanted to be arrested. An officer would yell out to the crowd, "If you want to get arrested, get over here and get on this bus. If you don't want to get arrested get over here." My mother had told me and my sister that we were not to get arrested.

My sister had been chosen to participate in a summer program in Winston-Salem for gifted students. It was an integrated program called The Governor's School. My sister was a talented artist. My mother thought her being a demonstrator, and especially if she got arrested, would interfere with her plans to attend the program.

We were also told that while we were marching, should we see my father who worked at the post office near the demonstration area, we were not to acknowledge him in any way. We didn't want him to get in trouble and possibly be fired because his family members were so-called troublemakers.

Even though demonstrations in Greensboro never got as vicious as some of the others around the country, there was always the potential for violence. We never knew what the white folks might decide to do. They never knew what the Colored folks might decide to do. What I didn't realize was how significant and powerful these peaceful demonstrations would prove to be. In the beginning I didn't understand how marching was going to change anything. Greensboro became a city that was "heard around the world." The world watched, and many cities staged sit-ins and demonstrations based on Greensboro's model.

Many years later—in the 80s, when my children were young, they were performing in a dance concert at the Carolina Theatre. The theater, which was originally opened in 1927, had gone through a few renovations by this time. When I took them to rehearsal, we entered through the front door. I stood in the lobby with them for a second and then I walked out with them. We went back in again. I said to them, "I just came through the front door!" I turned around and took them out again. We came back in again. "We just walked in the front door of the Carolina Theatre." I laughed out loud. "I came in the front door!"

Me, Nervous?

I think about how the times affected my childhood—and my life. The nervous atmosphere and racial tension and how badly we wanted to have the same rights and respect as white people.

I suppose what I find most mind-boggling is that in all of my 30-something years of therapy and counseling, in and out of mental hospitals, in amongst the medication, during the depression and suicide attempts, through the periods of anger and frustration no one—not one professional—not one social worker—not one therapist—not one counselor—not one doctor ever asked how it felt to be a Negro, Colored, black child in the South during segregation, or how it feels to be black in America. To me that would be the same as treating a war vet for post-traumatic stress syndrome but never acknowledging he was ever in a war.

I was given my first tablet of Valium when I was fourteen. One day, I couldn't stop crying. My mother took me to the doctor. I must have been in terrible shape. We were not people who went to the doctor for every little symptom. My mother was from the school of, "Stop crying before I give you something to *really* cry about."

Funny, I don't remember why I was crying. I don't remember the details about what was going on around me on this occasion, but I do remember how I felt. I remember feeling very nervous and very scared. I was physically trembling. There was nothing specific at that time that I could pinpoint as the cause for me feeling so emotionally overwhelmed. Well, nothing more than any other day in my life at that time. I had never felt that emotional and uncomfortable before. And that in itself was causing me to feel even more nervous and more afraid.

I had always cried easily. I tried to be tough, but it just didn't work for me. My family used to say, "She'll cry if you look at her the wrong way." Sometimes people thought I cried on purpose for sympathy or attention. But believe me I really didn't want to get attention by being a crybaby. I was embarrassed that I cried so easily, and it made me angry to think that people would think I would make myself cry on purpose. Even today as an adult who feels I'm pretty much together, I still cry easily.

I don't like to see people mistreat other people. I don't like it when people mistreat me, and even though I've honestly learned to rise above mean comments and mean-spirited people, there's something about their actions that causes me to cry. It just all seems so unnecessary—being mean, or degrading, to someone else, and it truly makes me sad to see it. It wasn't until I was in my 40s that a therapist told me that crying is nothing to be ashamed of. Interesting, how I guess I always knew that, but sometimes we have to hear it from somebody else to believe it.

After that bottle of Valium, I never went back to the doctor or got any more. I assumed I was cured. The Valium did make me feel calm. I did get quiet and I stopped shaking. However, I felt woozy and emotionally and physically numb. I didn't feel anxious. I didn't feel anything. But oddly enough, when I wasn't crying, I was laughing.

Like my father, I developed a talent for making other people laugh. I got a lot of mileage out of that. I was popular, and a good student. My sister introduced me to the world of theater. My sister was in the drama class at Dudley High School. I thought she was a brilliant actress. I was impressed and excited when I saw my sister and the other students in a play called *The Night of January 16th* and then later in a show called *Our Town*. I thought Mrs. Wells, the drama teacher, was a genius at making these happen so seamlessly. I felt transported to another world and was instantly in love with the art of the theater.

My sister started directing me in comedy monologues and I started performing them at school talent shows. When I was on that stage, nothing else in the world mattered. In fact, there was no other world. However, it wasn't until I went with a group of students from my all-black high school to see a production of *Macbeth* performed by guest artists at a local university, that I knew that no other profession would satisfy me.

All of the performers were white. Or, at least I thought they were. Then I noticed that one of the witches was a black woman. I leaned forward in my balcony seat. I smiled and thought to myself, *"There is a Colored woman doing theater with white people in a real theater."* I wanted to be her. It was at that moment that I decided to be an actress.

I'm not sure how she got it, but my sister had this album with the soundtrack of the original Broadway production of *West Side Story.* There was a period of time when my sister and I played that album over and over and over again. We took turns acting out various characters and singing along with and mouthing to the songs.

I had never seen *West Side Story* at that time. There were a few pictures on the album cover. However, I had great hours of joy listening and imagining what the scenes must have looked like. Sometimes my sister was Tony, but I think I enjoyed being Tony more than she did. It brought me such joy to listen to the actors sing.

I mention this because little did I know as I pretended to be Tony and danced around the living room of our small house in Greensboro, that I'd not only meet the actor who was Tony on that album, the late Larry Kert, but I would also perform and travel with him. Mr. Kert joined a tour of *Two Gentlemen of Verona* that I was on. He was wonderful and funny and I loved being on stage with him. His time with the show was cut short after he did a back-flip during the curtain call one night, landed wrong, and hurt his leg really badly.

I was in the 11th grade at Dudley High, when I read about a new School of the Arts at New York University. I had never heard of New York University, but the article caught my attention because it said that at this performance art school, the emphasis was on performing. The article went on to say that the students were not required to take math or science. I was sold right then. I immediately wrote the school a letter and told them about how much I loved acting. I told them about all of the school and community shows I had been in. I had even been in some community shows with white people.

I was the first black child to ever be in a production of the children's theater at the University of North Carolina at Greensboro. I played the part of a bill collector in *Mr. Popper's Penguins*. I was kind of disappointed on the day when we were told to come to rehearsal early so that we would have enough time to put our make-up on. When it was my turn to get made-up, the director, one of the adults in charge of the play, said, "People with skin like yours don't need stage make-up."

He tried his best to make it seem like I was special. But, I felt that he was saying that, because he knew that some of the white parents might have a fit if they ever found out that the same brush that had touched a Negro's face had touched their child's face too. Or, it could have been that they just didn't bother to order any make-up that was dark enough for me. Whatever the case was, I thought it was a mean thing to do to a child, but I pretended like it didn't matter to me.

I told the people at NYU how I taught acting at the local community center and directed little children, who couldn't even read, in plays. I told them that a friend (I'll call him JoJo. He didn't want me to use his real name) and I were billed as the "best comedy team in the southeast" and that we had just won the Knights of Columbus Talent contest at the Greensboro Coliseum with a comical, musical rendition of *Goldilocks and the Three Bears.*

In my letter to NYU, I told them that I also wanted to be a standup comedienne like Phyllis Diller or Joan Rivers and was creating new material every day. And, I told them that I had just become the first chairperson of the newly formed Greensboro Drama Commission.

The Drama Commission was a committee of students who loved the theater and wanted to promote the arts in our community. The Drama Commission was unique in that it was a city organization made up of black and white students. It consisted of representatives from all the white high schools in the city, as well as the/my all-black high school. Things were changing.

NYU sent me some information back saying that I needed to arrange an audition. The closest audition city to me was Washington DC. I was already

ready. One of my scenes would be from the *Glass Menagerie* and then I would do a monologue as one of the witches in *Macbeth*. I was rehearsing every day.

Imagine me in New York City studying with the pros. I got all my letters of recommendation, wrote my essay, and filled out all the forms and was ready to send my application in. "Hey, NYU, make room for me 'cause here I come!" There was just one problem that I discovered in the fine print as I was about to put the application in the manila envelope.

One Hundred Dollars Please

I read it and I know my heart stopped. I'm not sure for how long, but I swear for a moment I felt like I would die. How come I didn't see this before? In disbelief, I read it out loud. "Please enclose a non-refundable $100 application fee." I threw the papers up in the air. "One hundred dollars! One hundred dollars? Why don't they just make it one thousand or one million dollars?"

I asked my mother and father if I could have the money. At first, they just giggled. Then my daddy made some comment that I didn't hear and they started belly laughing. My mother was laughing so hard she was holding her stomach and tears were rolling down her cheek. In amongst the laughter, I would hear one of them say, "a hundred dollars?" My father was laughing so hard that he couldn't control his hands long enough to even light his cigarette. I had to walk away.

After a few weeks of trying to explain to my mother how important this was and how there was no way I could lose, my mother went to a loan company and borrowed the $100. She said it was because she just wanted to shut me up because I was getting on her nerves. I know in my heart it was because she believed in me.

I went to the audition in Washington DC. It was the first time I had ever been out of the Carolinas. I went by train. My sister Roberta was attending Howard University in DC as an architecture major, so they asked her to watch out for me. She did.

It wasn't too long before I received the letter saying, "Congratulations, you have been accepted into New York University School of the Arts." I didn't sleep for a week. A few weeks later I received more paperwork from the school explaining how much financial aid I qualified for and how much money I would have to come up with. My heart stopped again.

Even if I added all the money that my father made as a mail handler for the Post Office and all the money that my mother made as a nurse's aide at L. Richardson Hospital each year, it wasn't enough. Even if my father stopped spending so much money on cigarettes and wasting money on alcohol and lost weekends, and actually paid the bills on time, there still wouldn't be enough.

I gave up on NYU and decided that I would go to Howard University too. It was much less expensive and I qualified for grants and loans that would practically pay for everything. But I secretly knew that as soon as I left North Carolina, I would figure out a way to get to New York City.

Tips Are a Good Thing

I was enjoying my last year of high school. It was during this time that I was working as a bus girl at Tex and Shirley's Pancake House in the evenings and weekends. So, I had my own money now. My mother and Aunt Thelma had taught me how to sew. I loved creating my own style. With the money I made I bought fabric and created outfits that no one had ever seen or would ever see again.

I discovered false eyelashes and wore red powdered rouge sometimes. I was not comfortable with boys sexually, so I was not a whore. I just looked like one—sometimes. Most of the time, however, I was clean, decent and respectable and wore my skirts and dresses at a proper, respectable length. As I recall, girls were not allowed to wear pants to school. Except for my band uniform and clothes I wore to play in the snow, I can't remember ever wearing pants.

When I started high school, I got a job at the pancake house. Miss Shirley and her husband owned and ran Tex and Shirley's Pancake House. I responded to an ad in the paper that said they were looking for a waitress. I don't know why I was attracted to that particular job. My family and I never ate there, or at any other dining establishment for three reasons. First, there was that segregation thing, so we weren't welcome at a lot of places. Second, my mother preferred cooking her own food and thought hers tasted better (and so did I). And third, it was just less expensive to eat at home.

I went over there and applied for the job. I'd heard about waitresses and tips, and tips sounded like a good thing. When I met Miss Shirley I liked her right away. She was a real nice looking white woman wearing, what I thought then, was a really beautiful red and white checkered dress. She had jet black hair that was teased and sprayed in a manner that made it stand up in a big round pile on her head and a real, southern, friendly, soothing way of talking. I guess Miss Shirley liked me too. I was hired on the spot.

She told me she was happy to hire me as a bus girl for now because they had just filled the waitress position. However, as soon as another waitress position opened up, I would be first in line. Well, I was the best bus girl ever! I was the only bus girl there. I was faster, cleaner, neater, and more polite than all the bus boys put together. Over the next few months, I saw a couple of new waitresses come and go. I was friendly with all the waitresses. The first few times I didn't say anything, although it bothered me. I kept thinking that Miss Shirley would say something to me, but she never did.

One afternoon, while wiping down a table, I overheard a conversation Miss Shirley was having with a woman that let me know this woman was about to be one of our new waitresses. I wanted to cry. I went to the bathroom to get myself together and then went to Miss Shirley's office. "Miss Shirley," I said. "I thought I was going to be a waitress next time you needed one."

Miss Shirley didn't say anything for while, she just looked at me and I just looked at her. Then she stood up from her desk, and looked up at the ceiling, and then down at the floor as if trying to find the right words. Then finally she said in a real soft tone and heavy southern accent, "Some of my customers won't understand. Some of my customers won't like it."

I don't remember if I cried. I wasn't angry with Miss Shirley. I was angry at the world. That was my last day working at Tex and Shirley's pancake house. I never went back.

A few days later, I was a waitress at Hot Shoppes. And, that is where I spent my last summer in Greensboro before going to New York City. The 6.00 a.m. to 2.00 p.m. shift. And, just as I had suspected—getting tips is a beautiful thing.

Groovin'

I played clarinet in the marching band at Dudley High School. That was the only reason my mother let me go to all of the football games in the evenings. I liked marching in the Christmas parade. That was the only time black folks got to take over the streets in Greensboro and feel like we owned them.

There was no band in town that could outshine the Dudley High School or the A&T College marching bands at the Christmas parades. Oh, I loved marching to the Dudley drum cadences. We were instructed to 'dress right' (let the person on your right be your guide for keeping the line straight), stand tall, proud and erect. Then we'd lean over—just slightly—from the waist while stepping high and fast.

The first car we owned was either a 1957 or 1958 red DeSoto. I loved that car. It was long with pointed fins in the rear. Each fin had a column of three red tail lights. My granddaddy gave the car to my mother. However, Roberta was the first one in our family to get her driver's license.

One Saturday when Roberta was driving me to my Girl Scout meeting, a man ran a stop sign, hit our car and we had no option but to smack into a cement wall. Roberta, my brother, Joel who was also in the car, and I were rushed to the hospital in an ambulance. All of us were okay, but the car was just a pile of twisted metal. For a few weeks after that, every adult I saw would say, "Y'all are so lucky to be alive."

I wanted to cry when I saw our new car. It was a dark blue 1963 Chevy Bel Air. It wasn't fancy or special like the DeSoto. It didn't have fins or pushbutton transmission controls—and it wasn't red.

I could usually get use of the car on the weekends. My friend Frances and I were experts at crashing parties. However many parties there were on any given Saturday night, we would make it our business to be seen at all of them. (That is, all of the party's given by Colored people).

Gas was 25¢ a gallon. So, if we could come up with $1.00 (it was sometimes difficult but we always did) we would ride around all night. I liked Frances. She was not my best friend. I was too independent— too much of a loner—too impulsive to have a best friend. But if I had had one, it would have been Frances. She was smart and funny and stubborn and resented authority—just like me. We laughed a lot and we vowed that we were going to change the world.

In between *Groovin' On A Sunday Afternoon* with the Young Rascals, *Sitting On the Dock of the Bay* with Otis Redding and *Feeling Good* with James

Brown, and learning all the choreography to The Supremes' *Stop In the Name of Love* and calling my friends whenever somebody Colored was going to be on TV, I found time to pay my respects to my neighbors and friends who were losing their sons and brothers and fathers to a war in Vietnam.

Girl, You Better Straighten Yo' Hair

Somewhere in the midst of these times, I started hearing the phrase "Black is Beautiful." I saw pictures and read about Colored people in some parts of the country who wore their hair nappy on purpose. Some Colored people were starting to call themselves black. They said that they were not Colored people. Let me see. I remember being called Negro, and I don't know exactly when it happened, but Negro became an unacceptable word. I was then called Colored. I was a Colored girl. Now, I was hearing that I shouldn't call myself Colored. I was Black. I was a Black girl. I was a Black American.

My community was not ready for that yet. I remember the day two girls showed up at high school with what they called "Afros." All hell broke loose. They were sent home with the threat of being expelled. They were told that they could not return until they straightened their hair.

I had spent most of my life trying to get my hair straight enough and looking forward to the day when I could afford to buy Nadinola skin whitening cream for myself. Didn't guys like the girls with long straight hair and light skin? Didn't white people treat you better if you looked more like them? At the time, I didn't have a choice. My mother, our school, and the city in general did not approve of "Afros" and that "Black" thing.

In the spring of 1968, two months before my graduation, Dr. Martin Luther King, Jr., was assassinated. Following the news of King's murder, racial violence broke out in cities all over the country. New York University was forced to adopt a new Minority Recruitment Policy and I was one of the minorities recruited. The very day before I was to leave for Howard University, I received a telegram from NYU informing me that I would be given a full tuition grant to New York University to study acting.

"Ma! I'm going to New York City!"

"Stay out of Central Park. Stay away from Puerto Ricans." (Interesting advice from a woman who, to my knowledge, did not know anyone who was Puerto Rican and hated that she was stereotyped because of *her* ethnic roots.) "There are some women that like other women." This was the final advice my mother gave me as my father lifted my suitcase onto the train as it was pulling out of the Greensboro station heading for New York.

I moved to New York City. I was an acting major at New York University. Ever since I'd read about the school in a Seventeen Magazine I knew this was where I belonged. I already knew before I even read that article that I belonged in New York City. I don't know how I knew. I just knew. From the books and magazines and TV shows I saw about New York—I could sense the energy and the excitement. And of course the theaters—I wanted to be where Broadway was. I wanted to be on the Johnny Carson Show. The Tonight Show, my favorite TV show, starring Johnny Carson, was originally produced in New York City.

The first Broadway show I ever saw was *Hello Dolly* starring Pearl Bailey. It was all so grand! All of the men and women in the show were so beautiful.

The music was brilliant and I thought the performances were fabulous. I could not believe I was seeing Pearl Bailey live and in person. My father had all of her records. When I was growing up in North Carolina I listened to her almost every day. And now, here I was in New York City, in a Broadway theater with the magnificent Pearl Bailey.

On weekends, I worked as a waitress at the Howard Johnson's on Sixth Avenue in Greenwich Village. (Yes, I was a Ho Jo girl). I was a terrific waitress. I was so good that I would order a customer's meal for them before they even got to the restaurant. If you were a regular customer and I looked out the window and saw you making your way to the restaurant, I would just go ahead and get your order started.

One Saturday, two young boys came in and sat in my section. They only had a few dollars. They asked me what they could get with the money they had. I worked it out so that they could each get a hotdog, a soda and an order of fries to share. When they left, a man from another table gave me a $10 bill. He said he thought it was great how I served those boys knowing that they didn't have any money to tip me.

I loved my classes. I had acting, speech, theater games, circus, and dance. There was a lot going on at NYU—and in the world. I called my teachers by their first names. I went to bars with them and my classmates. For the first time in my life, I could go and come as I pleased.

Of course, against the advice of my mother, one of the first things I did was go to check out the *dangerous scary overgrown* Central Park where people were killed, mugged, and raped. According to stories I'd heard in North Carolina, these were the main activities that took place in Central Park.

I was pleasantly surprised. It was so beautiful. The hippies hung out there and had love-ins and be-ins. There were music concerts, lots of green grass, and the smoking kind too. In fact, there was so much marijuana around my school that I really believed marijuana was legal in New York. I had never been around any kind of drugs in Greensboro, or if I had, I didn't know it. Because my father was an alcoholic and I saw what drinking could do to a person, I'd vowed that I would never do that.

I did not stay away from Puerto Ricans. I was fascinated with their culture. I wished I'd been more diligent in Spanish class so I could communicate better. I wish someone had told me how important knowing Spanish would be if I was going to live in New York City. I loved how passionate Latinos were— and how high the heels were on the shoes some of the women wore.

I also know I spent time with women, who as my mother said, "like women." It was not an issue to me then, and is not an issue now. I loved being in such a diverse city. I met people from places I'd only read about in my school text books. I met others from places I'd never heard of and could not even imagine what their lives in their native countries must be like.

When I stepped off the train at Penn Station for the first time in New York City, I had never smoked a cigarette, never done any type of illegal substance, had never drank even a beer, and I was a virgin. I had chemically-straightened hair that I kept curled in big, loose curls. I wore outfits that matched, and was overly polite and overly naive about everything— especially about men and sex.

I had never gone to school with white people before. The year after I graduated was the year that all the schools in Greensboro were finally integrated. Funny, but it wasn't the white people who got on my case. The black militants on campus didn't see me as black enough. I was constantly asked about my hair and when I was going to get an Afro. Some of the really militant ones were always inviting me to meetings to discuss what we should do to this white institution—NYU.

I was very happy to be at that white institution, and never quite got what it was I was supposed to be upset about, although I was afraid to say so. So, sometimes, I would go to the meetings just so the black people could see me there and would leave me alone to my acting and scene rehearsals. There was a time when I was invited to a meeting where all of us black students who were on grants and scholarships were being pressured to let the great white institution know that we did not want their money.

They said we should leave NYU because they were still in a lot of ways contributing to degradation of black people all over the world. I wasn't about to give up my money, but I didn't want them in my face either. Sometimes the looks they gave me as I would enter my dorm, Weinstein Hall, were really frightening. Then lo and behold I found out that most of these guys were not even NYU students.

I think my saving grace was that my roommate at Weinstein was a black girl from Long Island whose name was Benny. My name at the time was John.

I was glad Benny was my roommate because she was as dorky as me. I mean we just weren't 'hip'. We didn't know how to curse. We sounded silly when we tried. We didn't do drugs. We had straightened hair and dressed in clothes that fit and matched. We wanted to be part of the 'in crowd'. The popularity I did enjoy, I gained because I was funny. I had a great sense of humor and the gift for a funny come-back when one was needed. I could always liven up a party.

Even from grade school, I always loved a good party. Now that I was on my own at NYU, I started going to bars with my friends because I thought it was such an exciting thing to do. I tried whisky sours and daiquiris. Rum and coke was my least favorite. I tried a martini and scotch on the rocks. The scotch tasted awful but it gave me a buzz faster. Every weekend I would buy a bottle of J&B Scotch. I'd drink scotch before I went out to whatever party we were going to that night. So much for, "My father was an alcoholic, I could never do that."

But one Saturday night I drank so much I had a really bad hangover the next day. I had to work at the restaurant and I'd never felt so awful in my life. I'd never had a hangover before. I vowed this would be my last. I stopped drinking. It wasn't fun anymore. It would be years before I would ever have another alcoholic beverage.

I met Rudy at Ho Jo's. Rudy worked in the kitchen. He was tall—over six feet, had a big friendly smile and was real pleasant. He said he liked me and he invited me over to his apartment one day after work. I was still getting use to the idea that I could go anyplace I wanted without asking my mama. I liked Rudy and we had a lot of fun at the restaurant. That was the first time I had ever been in bed with a man. He was real nice and gentle.

Then he told me he was married. "But we are separated," he said. I suddenly felt so uneasy. I was in bed with a married man. I just felt so guilty and ashamed. "But we are separated," he kept saying. I put on my clothes and got out of there as fast as I could. Me and Rudy weren't tight friends anymore. I couldn't look him in the eye anymore.

I loved exploring the city. There was always something new to see and do.

However, I seldom if ever ventured north of 72nd Street. I had never been uptown to Harlem, and was scared to go up there because I bought all of the propaganda about the violence in Harlem and the drugs and the Black Panthers and the Muslims.

It would be years before I would realize that in many ways, the Black Panthers were one of the best things that ever happened for many black communities. The Black Panthers were organized out of a need to protect the black communities from unfair politics and laws.

The Panthers organized free breakfast programs in many communities across the country. They provided health programs and even a free ambulance service for black communities in Winston-Salem, NC. In other words, the Black Panthers were serving people and communities whose needs and concerns were not being addressed. It was the infiltration of non-supportive people and the media who so badly wanted to discredit this organization that made gullible people like me believe so badly of them. Years later, I would join the Nation of Islam and see first hand how the media can spin a story.

One Saturday afternoon, I had just finished a tap-dancing class at Clark Center for the Performing Arts, which was located somewhere on Eighth Avenue in the 40s or 50s. I was walking down Eighth Avenue on my way to the subway when this Yellow Cab pulled up beside me. I didn't look up. I just started walking faster. The taxi stayed right with me. "Hey. Hey girl. Oh, you're trying to act like you don't know me now." I looked into the taxi. The driver was this guy who was always hanging around the dorm. I said, "Hi," and I kept walking. The taxi was still with me. "Do you want a ride?"

"No. Thank you."

"See, that's what's wrong with you sistas. Every time a brother try to do you a favor, you give 'em attitude. I'm not goin' charge you. I'm going that way anyway."

The warning flashed in my head—the warning about getting into cars with strangers. But, he wasn't exactly a stranger. I saw him almost every day hanging out in front of the dorm. He was always at every party, meeting, and rally. One afternoon when I was eating dinner in Weinstein Hall, he had stopped by my table and told me his name. I didn't remember it, but he was certainly not a stranger. I said, "Okay. Cool." We drove in silence back downtown. I broke the silence as he was passing Fifth Avenue. "Hey," I said. "The dorm is down there. Just let me out here."

"I know. I know. I got a letter I got to get in the mail today. Goin' to take it over to the main post office on 34th, so I'm coming back this way."

"Just let me out at the next corner."

"Look you don't trust me? I'm coming right back. Just keep me company a little while. I'm almost at my apartment. In fact, we're here."

As he was parking the car, I said, "Well, just be quick about it."

"I couldn't possibly leave you out here in the car by yourself. It will only take me a minute to get the letter. Come on with me."

He lived in a fourth floor walk-up. His apartment was kind of messy and I didn't feel comfortable there. I wanted to just stand by the door until he got his letter.

He grabbed both of my hands and pulled me toward him. He fell back on a mattress. I screamed and told him to let me go, but he whispered in the most menacing voice, "Shut up." I did. I struggled to get away but he was too strong. I was crying and pleading under my breath. He ignored my pleas and forced himself on me. When he had finished I pulled my panties up and ran out of the apartment and down the stairs.

I don't remember the walk home. I was glad Benny was not there. I took a shower. I didn't feel clean. I took shower after shower after shower after shower. What could I do? Who could I tell? Who should I call? I was too embarrassed and ashamed to tell anyone. I took some more showers. I couldn't get clean enough. What just happened? Who could I tell? How could I form my lips to say the words I would need to say to explain to someone what that man did to me in his apartment? Surely, this was not rape because he wasn't a stranger. He wasn't a stranger. I took another shower.

I don't remember the seasons changing. But suddenly it was Christmas. I was excited about going back to North Carolina for the holidays. I was anxious to see what Greensboro would feel like now that I had experienced New York City. I was also anxious to see what Frances was up to. My Grandma Beady was quite ill. So it was decided that instead of my coming to Greensboro for the holidays, everyone in the family would just meet at my grandmother's house in Goldsboro.

Because my grandmother was in the hospital it didn't seem like Christmas. I don't remember exactly what illness she had. I heard someone mention cancer and someone else talking about diabetes. Perhaps it was a combination of the two.

We knew she probably was not going to make it. I remember the last time I saw my grandmother alive. I told her about how tall the buildings were in New York City; I tried to explain what a 'hippie' was and I told her I was enjoying my acting classes. She could barely speak above a whisper. The last time she spoke to me, she asked, "Ann, when am I going to see you on TV?"

New Year's Day had come and gone. Classes at NYU were going to be starting again in a few days. My family and I agreed I should go back to New York since there was really nothing I could do down there.

I took a Greyhound bus from Goldsboro to Raleigh, and then another bus from Raleigh to Richmond, VA. In Richmond, after about a 45 minute wait, I got on the bus that would go straight into New York City. I was happy I had a seat next to a window and I was just trying to make myself comfortable when the bus driver got on the bus with a small piece of paper in his hand.

He stood up in the front of the bus and looked at the paper for awhile. Then he looked up, and with a heavy Southern drawl said, "Is there a John Ann Washington on this bus?"

This is odd, I thought. *How does he know my name? And why is he looking for me?* I raised my hand as if I were in class and he was my teacher. "I'm John Ann Washington." He looked down at his paper again. He appeared uncomfortable as he read straight from the paper this time. "Your grandmother died and they want you to take the next bus back to Goldsboro."

Most of the events surrounding my grandmother's funeral are foggy. Death was scary to me. I was afraid to look at her in the casket, but when I did, I relaxed because I thought she looked so beautiful. My mother and Aunt Thelma had picked out a soft pink outfit for her. I wanted to say something at her funeral. My mother and aunt thought this was a bad idea. They kept trying to give me aspirin as if that was going to bring me back to my senses.

I insisted that they add me to the program. At my grandmother's funeral I recited a poem I had written in her honor about the amazing journey I'd had with my grandmother and how we had come to a fork in the road and she had been called to take a different path. But because I knew her and had traveled with her, the rest of my journey would be extraordinary. I was very calm and everyone liked the poem. When my grandfather died, exactly six months after my Grandma Beady, my mother requested that I say something at his funeral too.

When we were leaving the church to go to the cemetery, Roberta and I were in the back seat of one of the funeral home's Cadillacs and the woman who was driving the car was trying to comfort us. We really didn't need or want comforting but she kept saying things like, "Your grandmother has gone home now." "She is at peace now." "You don't have to worry 'bout Beady because Beady is in His loving arms."

While she was talking, she burped, but she kept right on talking. Well, I thought this was the funniest thing that had ever happened in life. I told myself. *Do not laugh. This is a funeral. This is a funeral. Do not laugh. You cannot laugh.* But I couldn't contain it. So I tried to mask it. I tried to make my laughter sound like I was crying. When I started doing that fake boo-hooing, my sister lost it too. Both of us were rolling on the back seat of the car laughing out loud and trying to make it sound like we were really crying.

The lady driving the car thought we were really suffering. The louder we got with our fake crying, the louder and more determined she was to calm us down. She started preaching, "Beady is standing before the pearly gates. Your grandmother was a good woman. Beady is being fitted for her wings right now." I thought we would never get to that cemetery. When we finally got there, I was never so happy to get out of that brand-new Cadillac and walk among the dead.

I'm Feeling Nothing

When summer rolled around I chose to stay in New York instead of going back to North Carolina for the summer vacation. I signed up to be part of these theater and acting workshops which turned out to be more like some kind of psychological therapy group. We did do a lot of acting exercises. However, at some point in the sessions, we would all sit round in a circle and take turns baring our souls. We were encouraged to dig deep to get to the core feeling and to connect with the real person inside of us.

Someone might express anger with a parent, and as a group we would try to support them through the anger. We would ask questions that we thought might get the person to have a different perspective. Sometimes people would just give advice or share how they'd worked through a similar situation.

Sometimes the sessions got intense and there was yelling and screaming. Sometimes, people in the group were angry with each other. As I think back on these sessions, it seemed as though we were taken apart emotionally but never put back together. These sessions usually ended with a group hug. (Well, it was the 60s).

When classes started in the fall, I started a new job as a box office treasurer at an off-Broadway Theater. This was my first theater job associated with a professional theater. It was a great job. I was being trained to run the box office for the Negro Ensemble Company (NEC). At the time, the Negro Ensemble Company was the training ground and theatrical venue of the finest black actors and writers in the world.

I mostly trained and worked across the street at the Orpheum Theater where a musical called *The Me Nobody Knows* was playing. Besides getting to see *The Me Nobody Knows* (which I loved) whenever I wanted to, I got to see the shows at the Negro Ensemble Company. An invaluable perk. I worked for *The Me Nobody Knows* until the show moved uptown to a Broadway house. Due to under-funding, the NEC was unable to offer me steady employment. I worked as a box office treasurer at various other off-Broadway theaters.

Sometime in my junior year the depression I'd fought for so long finally caught up with me. Maybe I stopped fighting it, or maybe it was just too hard to fight. I was functioning, but just going through the motions of my life. I felt removed from my own life. I felt like I was not connected to me or anyone. I didn't necessarily feel sad. I didn't feel anything.

Everything seemed pointless. I couldn't remember why my coming to New York and attending NYU had been a big deal to me. What was the point—of anything? I, who used to be so excited and curious about everything and always eager for an excuse to party, felt tired. I gradually separated myself from my friends and spent more and more time alone. I didn't feel any joy. I didn't feel anything.

It got to the point where I really didn't want to do anything but I was afraid not to. I was afraid to stop, so I just kept going. I don't think anyone really noticed I'd changed because I kept going through the motions. I don't know how I knew to go to the student health services and seek some type of help. I really don't remember if there was a certain incident or not. NYU health services referred me to a psychiatrist who I was to meet with twice a week.

I don't remember her name and I'm sure she doesn't remember mine. She would sit opposite me and knit. Yes. She would knit during the whole session. She would ask me a question without ever taking her eyes off of her knitting. It was around this time that I was prescribed my first antidepressant. I gave that psychiatrist three chances. The third and last time I saw her she was still knitting.

My second year at NYU, I moved out of the dorm and into an apartment. I wanted to feel independent. I wanted to experience the joy of fixing up my own place. I also wanted a place to retreat to—

somewhere to be alone when I needed to. I rented a small studio apartment in the East Village on Avenue C. It was a very tiny room with a separate, very tiny bathroom.

I had fun decorating it. I painted the walls a real soft blue. I had a tie-dyed bed spread with lots of yellow in it and I hung multicolored plastic beads for curtains. I had a small butterfly chair with a leather cover, a small desk, dresser and TV and small mattress. That's all that fit in my miniature apartment.

The apartment was sunny and I liked being there. The building in general was in really bad shape. The locks on the front door of the main entrance were always broken. Paint was peeling off the walls in the corridors. There were robberies every now and then. I'll never forget the first Earth Day because someone stole my TV on that day. Without my even asking, I received a letter from the city saying they were lowering my rent. They said I was paying too much. They lowered my rent from $160 to $135 a month.

The next year my sister came to New York to attend Columbia University. We decided to share an apartment. We found a beautiful newly renovated apartment on Avenue A. It was huge with shiny hardwood floors and bright white walls. Each of us had our own room. My room alone was twice as big as my whole studio apartment had been. We paid a whopping $245 a month for that place.

Hollywood

One beautiful November morning I went to JFK Airport and asked an attendant behind the TWA counter what time the next plane to Los Angeles would be leaving.

"Three hours."

"I would like to buy a one-way ticket please." I told her. She gave me a ticket for a non-stop flight from New York City to Los Angeles, California.

"Do you have any luggage?" She asked.

"No."

I thanked her for the ticket and sat down to wait for my flight to leave. I felt so peaceful—like it was exactly where I was supposed to be. I was sitting there waiting with a crowd of people, but I didn't talk to anyone. I just sat, looked, and waited. All I had with me was my backpack with some dance clothes in it, a wallet with my charge card, some IDs, and a twenty-dollar bill.

If I had done what was expected that morning, I would have walked seven blocks down Avenue A to 6th Street before turning west, then walked the two blocks to 2nd Avenue and then into the New York University School of the Arts Building. I probably started out on that route, but I can't be sure. All I know is on that particular morning in 1969, before I reached the school, I had decided to go to California. I had never been to California and I didn't know anybody who lived there. Nevertheless, I had to go to California and I had to go then.

I remember getting hungry and buying a chocolate bar at a concession stand. Now I had less than twenty dollars, but that didn't bother me. Nothing bothered me that day. Nothing could harm me. Everything was right and beautiful and I felt fantastic.

One minute I was eating a chocolate bar in New York City and the next minute I was stepping off the plane in LA. It was so-o-o beautiful and so-o-o warm and there were palm trees. I'd never seen real palm trees before. And I saw that guy who used to be Gilligan on TV walking through the airport. Wow! I was in the land of TV and movie stars. I felt great!

I found a pay phone and called my sister Roberta in New York.

"Hello," she answered.

"Roberta, I'm in LA!" I shouted.

"What? LA? Are you rehearsing something at school?" Roberta was in total disbelief.

"I'm in Los Angeles, California. Roberta, it is so beautiful here."

I remember her asking me so many questions all at once. "What are you doing there? Why are you there? Who are you with? How did you get there? When are you coming back?"

"Don't worry. The weather is really nice and the palm trees are really beautiful. I am fine." I told her casually. And I did feel fine. I was in Los Angeles, California.

I went outside to get a taxi. I didn't know an address or anywhere to tell the taxi driver to go, so I just said the address I always heard in the movies.

"Hollywood and Vine please." I said with confidence. And we were off. I didn't know where Hollywood and Vine was exactly. The ride lasted a second and I paid the driver. I only had a few dollars left, but I felt too fabulous—too calm to be concerned about money. I wandered around the downtown area for awhile and then I started to get tired and thirsty. I saw a bar with flashing pink neon lights around the windows. I went inside.

There was a young black man at the bar, about my age—nineteen, but he acted much older and wiser. He bought me juice and food. I am sure I must have lived with him for my first few days in LA. I don't know what story I told him about who I was or why I was in LA with no money.

The whole LA adventure was like a dream, or maybe a nightmare. This is where things get tricky, remembering and not remembering. I was there physically, but not mentally. I was not living in the same world with everybody else. But, because I continued to walk and talk and look like I was among the living, I was treated as if I knew where I was and what I was doing—as if I really understood.

The guy I met at the bar, whose name I don't remember, wanted to be a singer like Tom Jones. He lived above a bar and he had nothing in his room except a bed, a cheap record player, and lots of Tom Jones albums. He was always singing Tom Jones songs to me. He was actually a pretty good singer. He made me laugh and I felt comfortable with him. Again, I don't remember how or why things were happening, but I left him and lived on the beach for a few nights. I lived at the Hollywood YWCA for a week or so, and when I left I couldn't pay my bill. The woman who was in charge was so angry.

"Why do you girls always do this? Why don't you young girls just stay home if you don't have any money? Everybody thinks they are going to become a famous star in two weeks!" She yelled at me but I was happy that she did. I felt good knowing I wasn't the only one who had ever done that. I checked pay phones for change, I ate a lot of popcorn—it was cheap.

I met a young woman named Linda at a bus stop one day. She gave me room and board in exchange for taking care of her two children while she went to work.

I'm not sure how I got the job, but I remember working at Robinson's Department store helping with inventory in the lingerie department. I made friends with some of the other girls who worked there and ate lunch with them, told jokes with them and felt like I was one of them. I don't know where or how I was living at the time. On New Year's Eve, I slept on a beach, thinking that was the coolest thing in life. Four months passed before reality set in and I realized I was not where I was supposed to be.

For the first time during my California adventure, I was afraid. *How could I have come to California with no plans and no money? What was I thinking? What was wrong with me? What had I done? I wanted to go back to New York City.* For the first time in four months, I thought about going back to New York City. I thought about my family, and North Carolina, and my classmates and friends I used to 'hang' with in New York. But, I was too embarrassed to call them. *How could I call them? What would I say? What must they think of me?*

I felt that if I could just get to the airport perhaps I could charge one more airline ticket. I didn't have enough money to get to the airport. In fact I had no money at all. I went to social services and told them my story. The woman I spoke to wasn't buying it and she told me that is not what they do there. "Have a good day," she said, as she waved me out of her cubicle. As I was leaving the building, a short white man came out of the next cubicle and started following me down the corridor. He stopped me just as I reached the building's exit doors.

"Young Lady!" He yelled in a whisper.

I turned to him. He reached in his pocket and gave me a bunch of bills. He said he had overheard me speaking to the worker.

"Please don't tell anyone I'm doing this, but I want you to get home." I thanked him and said I would send the money back to him.

He said, "That's not necessary."

He had given me enough money to take a taxi to the airport and eat a meal too. I was able to charge a ticket back to New York City. When I arrived back in New York it was business as usual. Even though I lost a semester, I returned to NYU. My classmates and friends thought it was pretty cool that I would just get up and go to California. They'd say, "Wow! I wish I had the nerve to do something like that." My sister would just look at me and shake her head sometimes. Shortly after I returned, I got a letter from my mother.

Dear Ann,

I am glad that you decided to come back from California. I am also glad that you did not marry that man out there.

I have enclosed a self-addressed stamped envelope so that even if you don't feel like writing, just mail the envelope back and I will know that you are all right.

Love, Mother.

My family told me in later years that some-where in the middle of my California trip, I flew home to North Carolina and announced I was getting mar-ried. They say they begged me not to go back, but I did. I have absolutely no recollection of this.

I have heard that the human mind has a way of protecting us from things we cannot handle. I thank my mind for that. Perhaps my subconscious was protecting me when it said to me, "Mail the envelope back and throw the letter away. You don't want to think about this."

I was actually starting to feel physically and emotionally strong again. One of the drama coaches at the School of the Arts was an actor and director named Lloyd Richards. He approached me in the hall one day and just looked so deep in my eyes that it still haunts me to this day. He said earnestly but gently, "When are you going to stop running?"

There were a lot of off-Broadway shows in the village. My sister and I started ushering for the shows on weekends. Most of the shows had two shows a day on Saturdays and Sundays. They all had different and staggered show times. For instance, *The Hot L. Baltimore* Saturday show times might be two o'clock and eight o'clock, while a show up the block called *Let My People Come* Saturday show times might be seven o'clock and 10 o'clock. Well, my sister and I figured out how we could usher for almost every off-Broadway show in the village on the weekends.

We'd go around and usher for all of the early shows—sometimes as many as three a day. We'd get paid three or four dollars per show. Then we'd go back around to all the theaters and usher for their late shows and collect another three or four dollars per show. The best part was at the end of the night, while walking back to our apartment, we'd spend some of it in the village on cheap jewelry.

I enjoyed hanging out with my sister. She had moved to New York to work on her master's degree in architecture at Columbia University. We both loved the theater and enjoyed the same types of music. We saw a lot of Broadway and off-Broadway shows. We also enjoyed live concerts at the Fillmore East and other venues in the city.

I started dating an NYU student who worked as a sound engineer at the Fillmore East. The Fillmore East was located in the West Village next door to the NYU School of the Arts. It was *the* premier concert venue on the east coast and almost single-handedly started the careers of what would become some of the biggest bands in the world.

He would get me in to see almost any show I wanted to see. However, I had to sit in a light booth that was no longer in use. One night I was sitting in the light booth watching Nina Simone perform when Jimi Hendrix shows up and sits in the chair right next to me. There were only two chairs in the booth. He had two young white girls with him who sat on the floor at his feet.

I didn't know what to say to Jimi Hendrix. What do you say to Jimi Hendrix? So, I didn't say anything. About half way through Nina's perform-ance, he asked if I had a cigarette. It just so hap-pened I was going through my period where I believed that smoking was a very dramatic thing to do. So I handed him a pack of Kools. He took a cigarette and gave the pack back to me. When the concert was over we both got up and went our separate ways.

One of the rules for students attending New York University School of the Arts was that we were not to audition for shows other than those being presented at the school. It was 1972 when I read an article in a newspaper that announced a show called *Godspell* was having auditions.

The article went on to say that each person who comes to audition should choose a parable from the Bible and present it so that it's funny. Each person was also to prepare a song to sing at the audition. I'd often thought about being a standup comic. I liked the idea of taking a parable from the Bible and making it funny. I decided to do it.

I knew we weren't supposed to go to these auditions, but it sounded like so much fun. Besides, I thought to myself, it's not like I'm actually going to be cast in the show. I'd never even seen *Godspell*. I got busy working on my monologue. The parable I chose was the prodigal son.

The day of the audition I went to the Promenade Theatre on Broadway. At this audition, all of the people who were auditioning sat in the audience and watched the others audition. I wasn't nervous or anything like that. To me this was great fun.

When my name was called I went on stage and took on the persona of a preacher. I adopted a tone in my voice and a way of pronouncing the words that sounded like a cross between the stereotypical Pentecostal and Southern Baptist preacher. I bellowed, "There was a man and he had two sons . . ."

I would pause and shake my head at intervals, as if I could barely get through the story because of how emotional it made me. I heard the audience laughing and that made me feel great. I went on and told the story of the prodigal son who left home and went to New York City.

I concluded the story by strutting back and forth across the stage as I said, "So the son said 'I will arise and go back to my father's house. For in my father's house there are many cans of Afro Sheen™ (In the 60s and 70s Afro Sheen was the most popular hair care product to help keeps one's Afro looking shiny, and healthy). Everyone laughed and had enjoyed my presentation. I thanked everyone and started walking off the stage to go home.

"Don't leave." I heard a voice say. "We'd like to hear your song now." I never even thought about the song. I didn't have a song. I wasn't a singer. "I don't have a song." I said. "Just sing anything," someone yelled.

"I don't know any songs."

"You must know something."

"No. I can't think of anything." And I turned to leave.

People in the audience started yelling out titles of songs to me.

"How about *Somewhere Over the Rainbow?*"

"No."

"How about the *Star-Spangled Banner?*"

"No."

"How about *Walk on By?*"

I had listened to Dionne Warwick sing this song hundreds of times so I thought I'd give this one a shot. I sang a verse or two and then I said, "Thank you," and started to leave again.

"Don't leave. We'd like for you to do some improvisations with us."

My eyes lit up like a kid on Christmas morning. I loved improvisations. I stayed, and did improvisations with some of the other people who where also auditioning. I had a really good time and felt a little sad when it was over. They thanked me. I thanked them and I left. By the time I got home, there was a message on my answering machine that said they wanted me to be in the Washington, DC production of *Godspell.* The message included an address I was to go to the next day to sign a contract.

I was so sure they'd made a mistake I didn't even tell anyone about the message or the audition. I'd never been to a Broadway producer's office before, so I decided to go. I knew once they saw me they would realize I'm not the girl who they thought they were calling. But when I got to the office, everyone congratulated me and told me where to sign on the contract. I was still convinced someone had made a mistake. So the only person I told about being in the show was my sister, and I swore her to secrecy.

After rehearsals started in New York, I was glad I hadn't told anyone about the job because I could not sing the song I was supposed to sing. Oh, the acting and funny stuff I was a master at. I was to sing the one song in the show that was accompanied only by an acoustic guitar.

By My Side was not written by Stephen Schwartz who wrote the other music in the show and would go on to write music and lyrics for many incredibly successful shows which include *The Magic Show, Pippin* and *Wicked. By My Side* was written by Jay Hamburger and Peggy Gordon. Peggy, who was a member of the original cast, had a beautiful lyric soprano voice. I did not.

I was sure I was going to be fired because I could not sing that song the way she did. The cast was outstanding. They were genuinely friendly and amazingly talented. The hardest part would be saying goodbye to these wonderfully gifted people.

One evening after rehearsal as I sat in my Avenue A apartment trying to figure out how this *Godspell* scenario was going to play out, I was listening to a Nina Simone album playing in the background. And then all of a sudden it hit me. I turned Nina up louder. How would Nina Simone sing this song?

The next day at rehearsal I sang the song *By My Side* as if I were Nina Simone. It worked. But my troubles still weren't over. You see, I couldn't do harmonies. I usually ended up singing whatever the person next to me was singing.

New York rehearsals were over and we had moved to DC to do final rehearsals before opening night. It was the day before opening night. We were rehearsing when suddenly I heard Stephen Reinhardt, the musical director, say, "Stop!" He looked dead at me. "Miss Washington, what are you going to sing?" There was a short pause. Everyone froze. "We're going to sing every song in the show and I want you to sing whatever it is you're going to sing and we will build all the voices around you." Well, everybody was mad at me. I ended up singing the melody on everybody's song.

After the show opened I worked briefly with a voice coach and started understanding my voice. I took a few music lessons and gradually I was able to stick to my harmony on most of the songs.

I was in a hit musical show in our nation's capitol! I was making money! I was living in a high-rise apartment in Chevy Chase, Maryland. Life was good! However, when I accepted the role in *Godspell*, I breached my agreement with NYU. I was no longer an NYU student.

Hello Old Friend

I'd been performing in *Godspell* for a little over a year when the depression showed up one morning unannounced and in full force. During my time in DC the depression had paid short intermittent visits but I'd always managed to escape. However, this morning, it was as if it viciously attacked me and I didn't know how to get away. I surrendered. I felt numb like I was dreaming or sleep-walking. Time froze. I saw no past and no future; only that dark painful moment that had consumed me and that I thought *was* me.

How can I describe it? My soul ached—like an agonizing tooth ache—like a pounding head ache—my soul ached. I felt the only way to be free from this overwhelming sense of emotional pain and darkness was to die. I would have to die. I went down to the liquor store. Waited for it to open and then purchased a bottle of scotch. I washed down a bottle of antidepressants with a bottle of scotch.

Later that evening when I opened my eyes, I saw my sister and one of the understudies from *Godspell* standing over me. I was in DC General Hospital. I don't know how I got there, and to this day I've never asked. Surprisingly, after I woke up, I felt fine. I wanted my clothes so that I could go home. The doctors informed me that they could not release me. This is when I learned that people who make suicide attempts are admitted to psychiatric hospitals. Little did I know, this was only the first of what would become many psychiatric hospital admissions for me.

That first night there an orderly came around with a little cup of pills. "This is your medication." I took the tiny cup and poured the four pills in my hand and was about to throw them in my mouth. "No. No. Put the pills back." Now, he was whispering. I was totally confused and was wondering if he was really a patient too. But I did as he said. He took the little paper cup back. He tipped the cup so that I could see inside. He pointed to each pill. He continued whispering.

"Take this one and this one. Do not take this one or this one. Put these two under your pillow and I'll be back to get them later." I whispered, "I thought I was supposed to take them all." He pointed to two women that were in zombie-like states. One just stood motionless with her back against a wall, and the other woman rocked back and forth in a chair as she stared at the floor. "They take these." He said, as he pointed again to the two pills I was to leave under my pillow. I was still confused and I wasn't sure if I should trust him. I never took those two pills. I suppose it's because of situations like this, that in my later hospital stays, someone would watch us take all of our medication and made sure we swallowed.

The next morning at the hospital, I woke up in great spirits and full of energy. I organized exercise classes. I helped some of the ladies fix their hair. I had conversations with the other patients, told funny stories and actually had a good time. The staff didn't seem to mind that I was doing all of these things. It actually made their jobs easier. When medications came around, I always remembered to put those two pills under my pillow. I really wasn't sure why I was there. I rarely thought about the suicide attempt. And going into the third day, I still hadn't seen a doctor.

Of all of the unexplainable and unbelievable events in my life, what I'm about to share with you remains, in my opinion, right at the top. I do not even recall the details of how exactly I got this to happen. I was starting to get pretty restless on the psych ward. I was missing performing in *Godspell*. I don't recall ever missing a show until this incident. Berlinda Tolbert, who would later become well know for the role of Jenny on the TV show, The Jeffersons, was covering my role.

Somehow—and I *really* don't know how—who approved this—or who said what to whom—the hospital let me go do the show at night and then come back to the hospital. A man who worked at the theater would pick me up at the hospital a few hours before the show. I would leave the psych ward and go to Ford's Theater, put on my costume and makeup, perform in the musical *Godspell,* take my curtain call with the rest of the cast, take my costume off and then was driven back to the DC General psych ward.

After a few nights of this, I was discharged from the hospital. However, my doctor, whom I hardly ever saw, sent me to a halfway house and insisted that this is where I should live. A halfway house is a residence established to assist persons who have left highly structured institutions to adjust to and reenter society. I spent one night there and then I just left and got an apartment in downtown DC.

In a short time, I had my life back on the track. I was feeling good, just embarrassed about the whole mental illness and suicide attempt thing. There were some high school girls who ushered at Ford's Theater. Immediately after the show opened, they made it clear that they admired what I did in the show and wanted to support me in any way they could while I was in DC. They would watch the show over and over. I would joke with them that they knew the lines and lyrics better than I did. If I did something different in a particular show, one of them would say, "Why did you do it that way tonight?" or, "It was better when you said it the other way."

They called themselves my fan club. One of the girls, Vanessa Brown, often invited me to her home to have dinner with her parents. They were so cordial and the girls were so helpful.

I made a demo tape of some R&B songs with the musicians from the show. One of the high school girls, Brenda, asked if she could have a copy of it. One afternoon, Brenda called and said, "Turn on the radio." I turned to the station she told me to turn to. It was a popular, mainstream DC station. She said, "Keep listening." I heard my name and then they played one of the tracks from the demo. I started laughing. Brenda was saying, "Just stick with me. I'll make you a star!" Most of my embarrassment about the suicide and psychiatric hospital was because these young girls looked up to me and here I was being crazy for no apparent reason.

I was concerned about dealing with depression in the future. I found a new doctor. I thought I was feeling fine at the time. However, he thought I needed to be hospitalized for depression and a medication adjustment. So, I thought he must know something I didn't, and I went to the hospital again. This experience was totally different.

He sent me to a fancy hospital in Georgetown. The other patients there were doctors, lawyers, business people, politicians and other people with lots of money. It was so private that there was nothing on the outside of the building to indicate it was a hospital or treatment center of any kind. In fact, the outside looked like a hotel. I felt like I was at a resort. Vanessa would bring me all kinds of great food. My new doctor practiced out of here and I had really good insurance through my actors' union.

I was only discharged because it seems Blue Cross was not willing to pay for what they considered a 'country club'. So, I left and was ordered to continue to see my doctor as an out patient. His office was in the infamous Watergate Building.

I liked the new doctor. He had a great sense of humor. He told me that when he thought about being a doctor, at first he was going to be a gynecologist because he thought of all the possible things that could go wrong with the female body and he figured there was a lot of money to be made. He decided to be a psychiatrist he said, because he would get to sit down all day.

I was paying a lot for my sessions with him. I did feel better after I saw him, not because he did any so-called doctoring, but because he was a good person and he made me laugh. Then I got the notion that instead of paying him all of this money once a week to feel better, I could just come to Georgetown once a week to buy something pretty for less money and feel good. So that's exactly what I started doing.

I heard there was going to be a "Miss Black DC" pageant coming up. The winner, of course, gets to compete for the title of "Miss Black America." I wasn't doing very much besides the show, so I decided to join the competition. I was going to sing an R & B number. I hired the four musicians from *Godspell* to rehearse and play for me. Hillary, who was in charge of costumes at Ford's Theater, was a genius seam-stress and made a gown for me.

On the day of the elimination competition my sister came down from New York. I wasn't nervous because whatever the outcome was, I was having fun. I was excited. I felt good about my talent. When it was my turn, there was a slight pause while my musi-cians set up. The audience started booing my musi-cians because they were all white. It was the 70s. It was a Miss BLACK DC contest. I'd never really thought about my musicians being white until that moment.

These were the guys I'd been working with in *Godspell* for over a year, so it just seemed natural to me that they would be the musicians I'd bring to the competition. The audience was still booing when I was introduced and walked on stage. It was as if I was transported. I heard the booing but it did not affect me in the least. It was as if they were in one world and I was in another. I gave the signal for the band to start. I held the microphone close to my mouth and started slow and soft:

Do you want to dance?

Somewhere in the middle of the second line, the audience stopped booing.

Just when everyone thought I was ending the song, the band dropped out just as we'd rehearsed. I stepped forward and asked the audience, "You don't want to dance with me?" (I paused). It didn't matter what they answered. My answer was,

That's all right 'cause . . .

The band came back in—Two chords. I'd now switched to a more upbeat tune from the 60s—

I know! You don't love me no more . . .

I finished the song and left the stage to thunderous clapping and cheering. They even gave the band a round of applause. The woman who was after me refused to go on. I was selected as one of the finalists. Someone from McDonalds called the next day to talk about sponsoring me.

In the meantime, I got a call from a director in New York that I knew from NYU. They were putting together another touring company of a musical called *Two Gentlemen of Verona*. She offered me a role in the ensemble—a chorus contract.

I wasn't sure what to do. I was ready to leave *Godspell*. However, I knew I'd done well in the Miss Black DC pageant and was excited about that as well. After much consideration, I decided to take the show. I took the show because the chorus contract would at least get me back to New York where I needed to be to audition for other things. The Miss Black DC pageant seemed promising, but it could go either way. I wanted a new show. I now had a new show.

Love In the Air

I left *Godspell* and Washington, DC to embark
on a new adventure. Wow! *Two Gentlemen of Verona*
was such a fun show to do. It is a rock musical com-
edy based on William Shakespeare's play by the same
title. The cast was multi-ethnic, delightful and well, a
little wild. The show was originally produced by
Joseph Papp's NY Shakespeare Festival. After a
limited open-air run in Central Park, the show moved
to Broadway and received the Best Musical Tony for
1972. The company I was hired for would again have
a limited run in Central Park before touring the
country.

I loved the show. I loved the cast. I loved being
back in New York. Most of the cast would meet at the
Public Theater each evening and take a bus to Cen-
tral Park to get ready for the show. Some of the sup-
porting crew would ride the same bus. I met an actor
who was working that summer as an usher for the
show in Central Park.

Somehow I ended up sitting next to him most of
the time. He was tall, thin and had dark wavy hair.
His parents were from one of the Caribbean islands.
I'll call him Nick. Nick and I would talk all the way to
Central Park and then, after the show, talk nonstop

all the way back downtown to the theater. I started looking forward to sitting with him. If there was a party or some other special event that the cast of the show was invited to, I would end up going with him.

He soon let me know he was interested in me being his girlfriend. We started dating. I hadn't really had a lot of boyfriends and I was still dealing with the depression and I thought he was just too good looking for me.

My self-esteem was extremely low. I didn't know if I could handle a relationship where I thought the man looked better than me. However, he seemed to know all of the right things to say. He was friendly, and all of the ladies in the cast would say, "Oh don't let him get away. He's really cute and he's a nice guy too." He was charming. He seemed kind of shy at times. But I felt he really liked me.

When the Central Park engagement was over, the actress who played Lucetta said she would not be able to do the tour. The director asked me if I would like to play the role of Lucetta on the tour. She didn't have to ask me twice. "Yes. Yes. Yes." We started rehearsing and preparing the show and ourselves for the road.

I'm not sure how the conversation came up, but one day at rehearsal, one of the other principal actors asked me how much more I was getting to play Lucetta above what I would have gotten as an ensemble member. I told him there was no difference. He left the room. He came back a few minutes later and asked if I would speak to his agent on the phone.

The agent asked, "How much are they paying you to play Lucetta on the road?" I told him the figure. He told me to stay by the phone. In a little while he called me back. He told me they would have a new contract for me the next day. I would be making three times what the original contract was for. I waited for the agent to ask for his fee. When he didn't, I told him to please take it. He said, "Next time."

The first stop on the tour was Princeton, New Jersey. I will never forget that opening night as long as I live. It has become my favorite theater story. At a certain time before the show, the cast and musicians were to meet in a basement room so we could warm up musically. I was on my way down to the basement when I hear the stage manager call "places." One of the wonderful and unique things about *Two Gentlemen of Verona* is that it has no orchestrated overture. The Ensemble sings the prologue—a joyful sonnet about springtime love.

The show starts with a woman coming on the stage singing "summer, summer, I was like the summer, wondering where to go." (I was this woman when we did the show in Central Park). And, then another actor comes on stage singing about autumn. Another one comes out singing about winter; and the fourth actor sings about spring and suddenly the stage is filled with interesting and beautiful characters in fascinating costumes and a whimsical feeling is in the air. Cupid moves among the actors on stage.

As the opening night show is beginning in Princeton, I go down to wait in the wings. On this night as the show started, I heard the actress sing, "summer, summer, I was like the summer, wondering where to go." Then there was a long pause. "Hmmm, that's odd," I thought. "No autumn. No winter. No spring." I hear the Proteus Character on stage and he gives the cue for his first song. I don't hear the orchestra. I hear what sounds like one lone guitar strumming his song. "Ohhh." I said to myself. "That sounds awful. What is wrong with everybody tonight?" Much sooner than normal, I hear my cue from Proteus. I enter and say my line, "Que Pasa, honey?" Just as I finish, I notice a man making his way to the stage from the audience. He walks on the stage, tells us to stop, and asks that they bring the lights up.

"Hello. My name is Joseph Papp. Ladies and gentlemen, I don't know what's going on here. But, I intend to find out. This is not *my* show. So, take a few minutes and relax while I find out where *my* show is." We all left the stage. There was no orchestra in the pit, just a single guitar player. More than half of the cast was missing.

Oh, yea, the warm up in the basement! When I walked in the basement room, there they all were. They were having a good time laughing and jamming.

There were no monitors in the basement, so no one in that room ever heard the "Places" call and had no idea the show had even started. We started the show over again and this time it was pure magic.

Nick and I were still seeing each other, and when the tour was over we decided to move in together. When that tour ended I got a call asking if I would be interested in joining the Broadway production of *Godspell.* I joined the show playing the same role I'd play in the Washington, DC Company. It was my first Broadway show. My life was finally coming together.

I had a new boyfriend that I loved and lived with and I was starring on Broadway. After living with Nick for a few months, he started getting agitated over the least little thing. He was an actor, but wasn't working very much.

He wasn't a singer or dancer. He was exclusively a straight actor and the seventies was all about the rock musical. He would sometimes make comments that suggested I was not a real actor. That somehow to be a singer or dancer could not be taken as seriously as being a dramatic actor. In the meantime, I was bringing in all the money and paying all the bills all my 'couldn't-be-a-real-actor' self. Sometimes he said things that made me feel so worthless. But then, he would turn right around the next minute and be so sweet and gentle and loving.

We were married in our apartment on 54th street. My sister decorated and even converted the floor model TV to look like a beautiful wedding alter. The cast members from *Godspell* came and brought me a money tree. My mother and Nick's mother were there along with many of our theater friends. It was a low budget wedding; however, it was a happy occasion and a fantastic celebration with our friends and families.

I was happy to be a wife. I put aside the times he'd insinuate I was stupid or foolish, and the times when I would feel so confused because I couldn't figure out what he expected of me. For a while, it seemed like if I went left, he would say I should have gone right. If I went right, I should have gone left. But then he would apologize and be so sweet to me.

I remember one night the cast of *Godspell* was invited to the opening night of a new club. I didn't usually go to clubs, but this sounded like it was going to be an extraordinary adventure. Nick was going to meet me at the theater after the show and we would go together. When I didn't see him, I called him. He said he didn't feel like going. When I told him I would go with some of the other cast members, he said he really wished I'd just come home. "So, you'd rather hang out with your friends than spend time with your husband?" So, I went home and missed the opening night of Studio 54.

I was planning on visiting some friends in Washington, DC. Nick and I talked about the date. We both agreed that would be a good time for me to go. I went down to Port Authority to catch the bus to DC. There were unusually long lines and it was hot and crowded. The first bus filled up and no one knew when the next bus to DC would be leaving, so I decided to go home.

When I walked into my apartment and started for my bedroom I heard low voices. Nick was in the bedroom with another woman. Tears filled my eyes and my whole body was shaking. I left the apartment, went to a phone both and dialed my home number. I let the phone ring for what seemed like forever. I couldn't stop crying and shaking. I told him I'd been home and I knew he was not there alone.

"Get her out of my apartment!" I sat in a diner around the corner for about a half an hour. She was gone when I got back to the apartment.

"Where have you been?"

"Around the corner."

"Around the corner where?"

"The diner."

"So, why didn't you go to DC?"

"It was too crowded. I was tired. I didn't fell like going."

"Oh so you come back home to spy on me."

"What?"

"You said you were going to DC; you should have gone to DC. That's what you said you were going to do."

I remember two punches. One to my stomach and one to my face. The face punch hit my lip and I started bleeding. I fell back on the sofa. I couldn't move and I couldn't see for the tears. He walked away and had a cigarette. When I got up, I went to the bathroom and looked in the mirror. My lip looked really bad. I was horrified. I'm not a violent person. How did I end up looking like this? I got my purse and stayed in the bathroom until I heard him go into the bedroom. I opened the bathroom door as quietly as I could and bolted for the front door. By the time he caught up with me I was going out the front door of the building. I ran to keep ahead of him.

"Where are you going? Where are you going?"

The good news is St. Clare's hospital was only a few blocks away. I didn't have far to run. I ran into the emergency room door. And he was behind me. He slowed down and laid back when he saw cops in there. I was seen by a doctor right away. I needed three stitches on the side of my lip.

Nick was standing by the door of the treatment room. He'd told the staff he was my husband and was trying to find out what happened to me. A female police officer walked over to me. Her back was to him, but I was facing him. He was looking straight at me. The policewoman whispered to me. "Did he do this?" I shook my head yes. She leaned in closer to me, "Press charges. Don't let him walk. Press charges against him."

I looked at him. He looked so sad and lonely. He needed me. He'd never hit me before. I was confused. Press charges against my husband? I didn't know what to do.

"Don't let him get away with this. Look at what he did too you." Then the officer just shook her head, turned, gave Nick an intimidating look, and walked away. I went home with Nick. When I thought he was pretty calm. I told him I loved him but I didn't want to continue like this. I told him I was going to my sister's house. He begged me not to go. He said he would do anything just don't go. "I want to work this out. I'm sorry. If you ever loved me at all, then please give me another chance. I need you John-Ann." I made the mistake of looking up into his face—into those big sad brown eyes.

"Yes." I said, "We can work this out."

I got news about an apartment complex in midtown Manhattan near the Times Square area. It was intended to be luxury apartments for the wealthy, however, the developers went bankrupt and the wealthy were not interested in moving into that area at the time. The area was still somewhat of a 'red light' district—peep shows, prostitution and seedy night clubs.

There was an agreement between the perform-
ing artists union and the US Department of Housing
and Urban Development (HUD); Manhattan Plaza
became a source of affordable housing for performing
artists, other theater personnel and neighborhood
residents.

I was still doing *Godspell* on Broadway when
my application for an apartment was approved. I
remember walking into this magnificent, beautiful,
brand new apartment complex trying to decide which
apartment I wanted to live in. There were 43 stories
in one building, and 46 stories in the companion
tower. I chose a one bedroom apartment on the 7th
floor. The apartment included a large terrace. I was
happy about that.

Over the next few months the buildings became
home to many performing artists; the well-known and
the not so well-known. Between the two towers, the
complex housed Manhattan's only 50-meter Olympic
standard swimming pool and what was once touted
as the largest indoor-outdoor tennis courts in the
city.

Nick and I moved in. In order to qualify you had
to be currently working or prove the bulk of your
income was earned as a professional in your theatri-
cal field. There were also certain financial guidelines
that had to be met. Because of this, the apartment
had to be in my name because Nick did not meet the
qualifications. Nick had a few odd jobs, and every

now and then a promising showcase, but was not making enough money to support us.

That was not an issue for me. I was happy. I was making money doing what I loved. What was mine was his, and vice versa (I thought). Show business is unpredictable. An actors' employment status can change in an instant.

It seemed like we had ironed out all of our problems. I was having fun decorating the new apartment and meeting all of the new theater people who were moving into the building. On the weekends we usually went to someone's party. Usually it was to a party of one of his friends. He was not so interested in going with me to visit or party with my friends.

All of the women who knew him or met him thought he was extremely charming. He was Mr. Congeniality when we were outside. But at home, more and more he was critical of me, and seemed to know what buttons to push. I could wake up feeling great and within a few minutes of talking to him, I'd just want to go back to bed.

It happened gradually, but after a while, it seemed as if he didn't even try to hide his anger. I don't know what he was angry about. But somehow it was always my fault. One night as we were leaving a club we started auguring about something and he grabbed the gold chain I was wearing around my neck and twisted it so tight it left a mark. I remember packing a bag to leave that night and again he apologized profusely and begged me to stay.

I didn't know how to talk about what was going on with him and me. It was embarrassing. In fact, when I got the stitches in my lip at the hospital that night, I told everyone, including my family, that I fell off a horse. They knew I had recently gone riding with some friends and they also knew I didn't know how to ride and so I thought that was a good story.

My sister, who had lived in Mozambique for four years, invited me to go with her back to Africa for a visit. I was so excited. Africa. I'm going to Africa! Nick talked me out of that real fast. He even implied that since *Godspell* had closed I could better spend my time looking for another job. So, I did.

I played Prissy in a grand, musical production of *Gone with the Wind* in Dallas at the Dallas Summer Musicals. The original Broadway production of *Jesus Christ Superstar* happened about five years prior to the national tour I did that culminated with a short run on Broadway. I toured in a fabulous, clever and significant show entitled *Don't Bother Me, I Can't Cope.* It was an upbeat, yet powerful and poignant musical that dealt with the everyday life challenges of black people in America.

I wasn't rich and famous, but I did manage to make a steady living as an actress. I loved touring with all the shows, or "being on the road", as I like to say. My friends used to refer to me as the Queen of Bus & Trucks. Bus and truck tours were the Broadway show tours where the cast traveled by bus, and the costumes, scenery and props traveled by truck. The bus and truck tours mostly played one-nighters—every night a different town.

I did many of those tours and traveled all over the United States more times than I remember. I loved every minute of it. What a life. The hotels would be booked for you. Thursday night was payday. For Friday, arrangements would have been made for the cast and crew to cash our checks. For those of us who had a hard time saving, the credit union would take it out for us. Send money home, pay my bills and then shop, party and show up at the theater and do the most powerful and awesome show possible.

I never took a show or a performance for granted, no matter how many times I'd performed it. Each performance felt brand new to me. Performing was my lifeline. I wasn't depressed when I was on-stage. I did not have any worries or fears. I was someplace other than the everyday world. I was someone other than me.

I had a doctor in New York who would call in prescriptions for antidepressants if I felt I needed them. However, I rarely needed them. During the 1970s, drugs and alcohol were widespread in the theater. It was easier to get drugs than food. So, however bizarre I might have been because of my mental and emotional issues, I was considered normal compared to other people and their issues.

The Wiz was a huge hit on Broadway. A national touring company had already gone out. The first tour of *The Wiz* I was hired to do was a Bus and Truck tour. I was cast as Addaperle, the good witch of the North. The show was scheduled to be out for a year. Nick was starting to scare me with his unprovoked anger. The only time I ever felt relaxed and happy was when I was away from him and on the road. A year long tour was music to my ears. He didn't object too hard. Besides, I was starting to believe he was more interested in my money than me anyway.

I thought I'd seen and been in magical shows before, but for me there are no words to describe how blessed, honored, grateful and exceptional I felt to be allowed to perform in this show. This *Wiz* tour consisted of 27 performers, 2 dogs plus their trainer, 12 musicians, the conductor and company manager. The crew consisted of soundman, prop man, wardrobe supervisor, makeup supervisor, hairdresser, the production stage manager and the stage manager. This does not include the 34 extra local technicians hired in each city to assist in setting up the show and taking it down, or the 24 extra people hired to run the show.

My character would appear after the Tornado in a puff of smoke. I was an absent-minded Witch who attempted to perform magic for Dorothy. After a few funny lines, I would take the silver slippers off the dead witch under the house and give them to Dorothy. Then I'd sing a song to her about who the Wizard was and how to find him. I wouldn't appear again until the end of the show. I'd say a couple more funny lines, introduce her to my sister Glenda, and help everybody get Dorothy on her way home. Not a bad gig eh? I was a fabulous Addaperle.

I spent a lot of time backstage during the show. I became friends with one of the truck drivers who had nothing to do during the show either. He was an Italian guy from New Jersey. We told each other jokes and stories to pass the time. I liked spending time with him. It got to where if the show was going to be in a town for a few days, we would go check out the town or go shoot pool or something together. His name was Tony. He was my friend.

I'd been out with the show about 7 months when I finally made up my mind that I didn't want to be married to Nick anymore. He was jealous and was always calling to see what I was doing. In the meantime I was keeping all of our bills paid, plus sending him money each week for himself. The producers of the show, Tom Mallow and James (Jim) Janek, were really good people. I'd worked for them before when I did *Don't Bother Me I Can't Cope.*

As producers, they were fair-minded. They were not only interested in producing fabulous money-making shows; they seemed to be genuinely interested in the cast members too. One day I got a call from Jim Janek. He's sounding really jovial. "Guess what John-Ann?" he was so happy, he was almost singing. So I got happy too. "What?" "Nick is going to be joining you on the road for a while." I almost fainted, but I was still trying to sound cheerful. This was a big deal for a producer to do something like this. "Oh. Really? Why? Why is that?"

To this day I don't know what Nick told these producers, but somehow they got the idea that Nick and I were missing each other and them bringing Nick out to see me (at their expense) was a good and wonderful idea and would somehow please me. I wanted to die. "How dare he call my producers!" I thought. I couldn't find the words to say to Mr. Janek what I wanted to say. I froze. I said nothing for a long time. Then I said, "Thank you."

No one knew. I'd never talked to anyone about what was happening in our marriage. I wanted out now more than ever. I do not recall Nick's visit. Recently, as I was finishing this book, I asked a friend who was on that tour if they remembered anything about that. They told me Nick did come and it was dreadfully clear from my expressions and body language I did not want him there. As far as I was concerned my marriage was already over.

After he went back home, I partied more. I hung out later. When Nick would call, most of the time I didn't answer the phone. Of course he was angrier than ever about this. He started calling me at all hours of the night and morning leaving insulting or threatening messages. Still I told no one.

I lived each day to hear the overture of *The Wiz* and to enter coughing in that puff of smoke from down stage left. I was more than happy to point Dorothy toward *The Wiz*. When there were only a few weeks left on the tour, I made the biggest mistake I could have made. I told Nick from the road that when I got home I was divorcing him.

I think by the end of the tour, I'd confided in a few women in the cast about what I was planning, and what was happening with Nick. They couldn't believe it. "But he's so sweet," they'd say.

By the end of the tour, I was spending more and more time with Tony, the truck driver. I liked Tony. I liked hanging out with him. It was easy to be with him. I never heard him speak an unkind word to anyone. Even if he was angry about something, he seemed to find a way to resolve the issue without 'drama'. We made each other laugh and I could relax around him. He was not about trying to be cool or macho or hip. He was just being himself, and I thought that in itself was cool. We were a perfect match as far as temperament too. He didn't like arguments; I didn't like arguments. So, it was easy to fall in love with him.

As I sit here writing this almost 30 years later, I now understand Tony was the breath of fresh air I needed because I had allowed Nick to suffocate me.

Here was this gentle kind person who made me feel beautiful and wonderful. I could finally exhale. How could I not love him? I loved him deeply.

We were from totally different worlds. I was from the segregated south and he was from the north. I was black; he was white. I was from this southern Baptist background, and he was of this northern Italian Catholic background. So there was never a dull moment. There was always something interesting—something new to learn and share with each other. It was an exciting and happy time in my life.

The day I arrived back in New York, I was not only sad about the tour being over. I was sad about having to face Nick. I got to my building and I was sure I didn't want to go in to that apartment alone. I went to the local precinct and told them that my husband could get really violent sometimes and that I'd been away and things between us weren't good, and asked if one of them could go with me because I was afraid to go in by myself.

Two officers came up to my apartment with me. I opened the door. There was nothing there. All of my things were gone. My sister's furniture that she'd left with us when she went back to Africa was gone. All of my clothes were gone. All of the things I'd sent home from the road were gone. I'm not sure where I went but I didn't stay at my apartment because I was afraid of Nick.

Suddenly, to all of our friends, I was the bad guy. Because I never told anyone about his abusive ways, when I left, everyone thought I was being mean.

They were saying, "How could she do this to him? He allowed her to do her tours and this is how she repays him? By leaving."

"He is so sweet."

"He deserves better than this."

"She is so heartless."

I called Nick and asked him where my things were. He said he would tell me if I would agree to meet with him face to face somewhere.

I don't remember where I stayed at first. I eventually ended up staying with Tony in an apartment in New Jersey. Nick said he would not agree to a divorce, and just kept saying that he would be happy to give me back my things if I would just meet him so we could talk.

The first lawyer I retained just took my money and never did anything. After about four months, I found a new lawyer. During all of this time I refused to see Nick. The lawyer told me. "Do not agree to meet this man anywhere! You can always buy some new clothes and furniture, but getting a new face will be difficult."

The divorce only took a matter of months. Even though Nick said he was contesting it, the divorce went through because he defaulted by not getting some paperwork in on time. The apartment in Manhattan Plaza and all of the utilities were still in my name and I didn't know what was going on over there.

As far as I knew he wasn't working and I didn't want to be held responsible for anything. The last phone bill I paid before leaving the road was over $500.00 (this was the 70s). I had everything transferred out of my name into his. Months later I would ask myself, "What is wrong with this picture?" Answer: That was *my* apartment.

I was now living in New Jersey with Tony. It was a powerful relationship. We talked about our dreams and things we wanted to do in the future. Suddenly, nothing seemed impossible. There was no question that this was the person I wanted to spend the rest of my life with. This was the person I wanted to have a family with; there was no question about that. It all felt so right.

From the outside it may have looked really different, I mean, with the race difference and everything like that. But from the inside it felt good. And so I didn't even think about what it looked like from the outside, because after a while that didn't even matter. I could be with him and totally forget, yes, totally forget that he was white and I was black. When I was with him I just saw a person, a really exceptional, funny—cute person that I was both physically and emotionally attracted to.

With me being black and him being white, I knew it would be hard. But I guess when you're in love you just figure like you can conquer anything. That's how I felt and that's how I think he felt, too. We were two beautiful, kind-hearted people who wanted to have a beautiful life together.

I told myself, Okay. This is it. All that other stuff was just practice. This is the beginning of my new, real and exciting life. But I found out Fairlawn, New Jersey (where we lived) is not where you want to be if you are intent on having a new, real and exciting life. At least it wasn't where I wanted to be. We had a great, spacious apartment over a trophy store on Route 4 where we entertained our friends and shared lots of fun and love. Nevertheless, we both agreed this was only a temporary home. Knowing this made living in Fairlawn a little more bearable.

He was the oldest of five children. His father was Italian and his mother was German. His family didn't seem to mind that I was black and welcomed me with open arms. At least no one ever said anything to my face. I got along well with his brothers and sister and enjoyed spending time with them. Individually, each had a unique personality and was sensitive and smart. Collectively, they were a funny, unpredictable and wild bunch that made me laugh and included me in some exciting adventures. I liked Tony's mother right away. She was friendly, witty, open-minded and was easy to talk to.

If anything, Tony and his parents were too close. By now I was used to being independent from parents. His father seemed genuinely friendly to me. However, I was uncomfortable with the amount of influence and control he seemed to have over the other family members.

Tony started driving long distance trucks. I used to travel with him when he made long distance trips across country. I was collecting unemployment and deciding what to do next. We decided to move to Los Angeles, California. We both liked the idea of warmer weather, and I could get a feel for the television and movie industry. Tony was also becoming more interested in the entertainment industry. I was also thinking it would be good to put some distance between us and his father—like, a whole country.

We told his family about our plans to move to California. His parents had lived in New Jersey all of their lives. Members of his family rarely left New Jersey for any reason. Well...his family not only decided to move to California, but moved there before we did.

When Tony and I were ready to move, we drove across country to California. Before we actually started the trip west, we drove south so I could visit my mother and he could meet her. I knew the visit was going to be interesting. My mother had already suggested that we try to arrive at night so the neighbors wouldn't see me coming in to her house with a white man. My mother got her wish. Although we didn't plan it that way, it was already dark outside when we arrived.

When I rang the doorbell, it took her a while to come to the door. Knowing my mother as I did, I knew she was waiting before opening the door to create just a touch of drama. Before she opened the door, she pulled back the curtain and peeped at us through the door window. Then, we could hear her inside turning the locks back and forth as if she wasn't sure how to open the door. Finally, she slowly opened it and stepped back across the room so she could get a good look at both of us. I walked in first and Tony was behind me.

"Hey mama!" She looked at Tony from his feet up to his head and then back down again before she spoke.

"Well, come on in. Glad you could find the time to come by to see me."

"Mama, this is Tony."

"Nice to meet you Tony. Have a seat." She motioned for him to sit down on the sofa.

"You have a very nice home Mrs. Washington."

"Thank you." My mother's eyes lit up. My mother was extremely proud of how clean and beautifully decorated she kept her modest home. In addition, my mother had always been a sucker for flattery. Tony had scored two points. She, however, wasted no time with the same drill she had always given my friends.

"So, what do your people do?"

"Are you hungry? Ya'll can just come in the kitchen and help yourselves. I hope you like my cooking." We followed her into the kitchen. We ate chicken and collard greens, potato salad and sweet potato pie during an arsenal of questions.

"Where did you go to school? Did you go to college? How many brothers and sisters do you have? What year were you born? What church did you grow up in? Do you have benefits on your job?"

He could barely answer a question before she would throw another one his way.

Tony said, "You're a very good cook, Mrs. Washington. Did you make this pie yourself?"

"I sure did", my mother said proudly. "That is not a store bought pie. I make all my pies from scratch. I made that sweet potato pie from scratch." Now of course, my mother took great pleasure in explaining every detail of how she made the pie.

We said our goodbyes and Tony and I left shortly after a sweet potato pie cooking lesson. We found our way back to the interstate and drove for a long time without saying anything.

We turned our trip to Los Angeles into a sight-seeing excursion. When we arrived in California, we were in Northern California. The first major city we stopped in when we got to California was San Francisco. I'd been to San Francisco before with various shows. However, this time, after only being in San Francisco a few days, I fell in love with it and I didn't want to leave. I fell in love with the ocean and the hills and bay windows. There was something about San Francisco that was exciting but not overwhelming. Tony felt the same way. We never made it down to Los Angeles.

Oddly enough, this happened to be the same area where his family settled. They lived about an hour or so north of the city. While we looked for an apartment, we stayed with Tony's family. I was sorry to learn racism was alive and well in San Francisco. I would go to see an apartment and would be told it had already been rented. Tony would go to the same apartment a few minutes later and would be told it was still available. This happened on many occasions.

Finally, Tony rented an apartment without mentioning me. I got a job as a manager of a small antique photo studio on Fishermen's Wharf. This was a photo shop where patrons were dressed in costumes and set up with props to make it look like they were living in an earlier era. The photos were finished in sepia tone. There was a much larger antique photo studio right on the main street in the Wharf. However, this one was somewhat off the beaten path, but still thriving.

The owner was a photographer who I'll call Juan. He was married and was the father of two young children. I always got the feeling that he really didn't have to make a living and the antique photo studio was just something to do and somewhere to go. I treated his studio as if it were my own. In fact, most of the patrons assumed I was the owner because of the great customer service I provided and how protective I was of the shop and its reputation.

I'd worked for Juan off and on for about a year, when I told Juan that Tony and I had decided to have a wedding; he was extremely happy for us. His eyes actually twinkled. A few days later he told me he was impressed with the way I took care of his antique photo business. "For a wedding present, I'd like to give you $20,000 and help you set up a business of your own."

He told me to decide what I wanted to do and he would help me make a plan. He said if $20,000 wasn't enough, he would add more money if necessary. I was dizzy. Did I hear him correctly? I asked him to repeat what he said. I wanted to be sure I'd heard correctly. Who was this beautiful man! We also made the arrangements to have the wedding and the reception right in his photo store.

A Universalist minister I found from an ad in a newspaper was going to officiate. When we met with the minister my main request was that he just not say the word "obey" anywhere during the ceremony. Tony and I also agreed I would maintain my legal and professional name, John-Ann Washington. He, Tony and I decided it would be fun to get married in the vintage wedding costumes at the photo store. From the front the costumes look like real outfits. However, from behind you can see that the backs of the costumes are held closed with sets of ribbons that are tied together. The costumes slip right over whatever you are wearing.

It was a small gathering at the store for our wedding, just a few friends and family. Our dear friends Bill and Grace who we'd met on *The Wiz* tour, and were also living in San Francisco, came. My wedding march was a recording of *Going to the Chapel* sung by Bette Midler. Tony used a garnet and gold ring I already owned for my wedding band, and we had cake and plenty of champagne.

It was a few days after the wedding when I found out Tony's father had befriended Juan and convinced him that the $20,000 he was thinking of giving me would be better spent on his fledgling woodshop business. Tony said his father explained that by doing that, everyone in the family would benefit in the long run. Suddenly, I was depressed. The good news was, this time, I knew why.

To this day I don't know why my anger didn't force me to confront Tony's father. Did it have anything to do with my Baptist upbringing and living with Jim Crow laws and learning to be docile? Was that what the abusive relationship was about? Did I on some level still think of myself as a second-class citizen?

Tony and I augured about what his father had done. It was our first serious quarrel. What could I say to Juan? After all, it was his money. I couldn't tell him what to do with his own money. I have often wondered what Tony's father must have said to this man that he'd only known a few days to convince him to give him my $20,000. Did he lie and/or somehow give Juan the impression that I had agreed to this idea? How did he do that? Why hadn't my husband fought for me?

This incident caused a shift in my feelings and thinking about my new family. I'd been too open, too giving, too trusting. I had identified an enemy. Was Tony's father the only one? I put on an invisible veil of armor. This one incident would be at the root of every disagreement I would ever have with Tony in the future.

After a week or so, I was too busy and having too much fun to just worry about my $20,000 and Tony's father. I got a job in a children's theater company, the Twelfth Night Repertory Company that toured all over the Bay area. We wrote our scripts and own music for the shows. We performed shows for students of all ages. We would come up with the message we wanted to convey and then figure out how to get the message across with a lot of humor and audience interaction. Our main show was called the *Great American Wild Waste Show.* This show addressed the issue of how to be environmentally friendly. I was also taking English, writing and music classes at San Francisco Community College. Tony was taking classes in film and theater production.

We both wanted a child, so, we were totally thrilled when we found out I was pregnant. This was a happy time for both of us. I knew Tony and I would be great parents. I went through all of the normal parent-to-be anxieties. I liked my doctor. I read every piece of literature he gave me about childbirth and Tony and I joined a Lamaze class. I decided I wanted the birth to be as close to natural as possible. We'd already been told the baby was a girl. We made plans for our daughter to be born in the natural birthing room at San Francisco Children's Hospital. This was a room that looked more like a hotel room than a hospital room. No medications were to be taken in the birthing room.

The baby was due around the end of January. I was never sure if my doctor was joking or not when he said that if I went into labor on Sunday January 24th, don't call him. When I asked him why, he said, "Nothing is going to keep me from watching the 49ers beat up the Cincinnati Bengals in the super bowl." Marie has always been considerate. She waited until the following Saturday, January 30, 1982, before she made her entrance.

After we'd been in the birthing room for a few hours, I was feeling more pain than I expected. "Hmmm. What do I do now?" I thought, "I really would like some medication for the pain." However, in the natural birthing room there are no drugs allowed. "What was I thinking?" I wanted to go to a regular room where I could get regular drugs, but I was too embarrassed to say anything. Once again, Marie came through for me. The nurse didn't like what she was reading on the monitor. She thought the baby might be in some distress. She suggested that I go to a regular room so that they could monitor the baby better. I think she expected me to put up some resistance to that idea. I tried not to act too anxious to go. However, the minute I was in the new un-natural room, I begged for something to relieve the pain and I got it. Thank you, Marie.

Before she was born, we decided her name would be Alexandra. We would call her Alex for short. However, the moment she was placed in my arms, I said, "Hello Marie." I don't know where that name came from. It was not a name we'd ever considered. She just looked like a Marie to me. If you didn't know who her parents were, you would swear that one of them must be Japanese. She had thick straight jet black hair and two large shiny black marbles for eyes. I never wanted her out of my sight. Tony and I loved her and loved looking at her. She was breast fed and never had a bottle in her life. If I were ever away, she wouldn't eat.

It was as if Marie and I were still attached. Where I went, she went. If I felt a place that I wanted to go was not child appropriate or child friendly, I didn't go. We never talked 'baby talk' to her. We talked to her like the wonderful and intelligent being that she was. We enrolled her in baby gym, introduced her to a lot of different music and made her feel as welcome and as comfortable as possible.

I read a ton of books with rules on how to be a good parent, and then I threw the books away and broke all of the rules. I decided the simplest thing to do was to just treat my child as I would want to be treated. That was my rule then. That's my rule today, 26 years later.

From the time Marie was born, she was never on a feeding schedule. I believed that if she got hungry she would let me know, and she did. If she got sleepy she would go to sleep and she did. As far as raising a child, I did everything wrong according to the books and according to other parents. For instance, I could not stand to hear a little baby cry in the middle of the night. I know the rule is the baby has to cry and you can't run and take the baby up or the baby will get used to being picked up, and you spoil the baby. Well, I couldn't follow that rule. If I heard my baby cry I would go pick her up and comfort her every time.

If I had something to do the next day, I would be tired and sleepy, but I always felt good that I didn't let my baby cry through the night. I know to a lot of people this sounds like enough evidence (on its own) to lock me up in some institution. I'm glad I did it and would do it again. I would only hope someone would do the same for me if I should cry in the middle of the night. Eventually, she started sleeping through the night on her own and today, she is a loving, healthy and happy person.

Marie didn't eat sugar until other adults started giving her cookies and candy without my consent. The idea of spanking—hitting or tapping in any form, was never going to happen. I certainly did not want anyone to ever hit me again. So, why would I hit my own child? I was happy Tony felt the same way about spanking. She was a happy baby. No trouble at all and a joy to be with.

When Marie was about one year old, the three of us moved just north of the city to the town of San Rafael. It was sunny and beautiful there. I was a stay-at-home mom. Oh I loved it. I got to stay home and make a nice home for my husband and cook and take care of my little girl. Wow! Does life get any better than that?

Tony was working for his father at his father's woodshop. The strangest thing was, if his father felt we had money, his father wouldn't pay him. We'd have to be strapped and have bills due before his father felt it was necessary to pay him. Yes. Tony and I had heated discussions about this.

Happy as I was, before long I wanted to perform again and even explore the possibilities of being a comedienne. I decided I would put an act together, in which I would perform songs that I liked and include comedy routines and play various characters. The person who was doing the closest to what I wanted to do was Bette Midler. After seeing the movie *The Rose*, I decided I was "The African Violet." The bass player from Godspell, an exceptional musician, named Mac, was now living in the San Francisco area. I told him what I was interested in doing and hired him to help put a demo tape together.

Tony, who was acting as my manager, was as excited as I was about "The African Violet." I did a few gigs in some small clubs in the area. One of my most heart-warming memories is of Tony coming down to a club in San Francisco to see me perform. We had brought Marie, but she was not allowed in the club. When I was on stage singing, I could see Tony with Marie on his back in the back carrier outside on the side walk. They watched and cheered me on from the sidewalk that night.

We were just starting to think there were some real possibilities with The *African Violet* act when out of the blue I get a call from Jim Janek. They were putting together a national tour of *The Wiz*. The tour would be out about a year before playing Japan and then re-opening on Broadway. Stephanie Mills who originated the role of Dorothy in the Broadway production would star in this production.

He wanted to know if I was interested in being Addaperle in this new tour. I'd need a few days to think about this. He knew that Tony and I were married. I told him about Marie and he seemed genuinely happy for us. I told him I'd have to give this some thought. I wasn't going to leave Marie. In addition, there were a few people who were starting to show a little interest in *The African Violet*.

Tony had a minor accident and had to be in the hospital for a few days and was unable to work. On this one particular day, many members of Tony's family and friends that we didn't see often had all come to the hospital to visit Tony. At one point the room got quiet. Tony's father walks over to me and openly (so that everyone can see) shoves this wad of money into my hand and says, just loud enough for everyone to hear, "Take this money. I hope this can help you while Tony's not able to work."

First of all, he had a lot of chances to give me some money in private if he wanted to. Secondly, this was the money he owed us for Tony's work. Thirdly, when I opened up the wad of money it was a large number of small bills that didn't nearly amount to the money that was owed us. However, everyone in the room looked toward me and smiled. I'm sure they were thinking, *what a kind generous man to help this poor suffering young couple with a large gift of money.* This made my Wiz tour decision easy. It was time to put some distance between this man and me.

In the meantime, I'd sent Jim Janek a demo tape as he requested. When he called me back, I told him I was ready to go. "Mr. Janek, how can we make this work?" He helped me devise a plan of how I could do the tour and not leave my child or my husband behind. Marie and Tony would come with me on the tour. Tony would be Marie's official nanny. We got out of our apartment lease and went to New York for rehearsals. It was good to be back in New York City, and even better to be working as an actress again. I was happy to have my family with me. I was excited for Marie. This two year old was in for a thrilling experience. I was excited about experiencing 'the road' through the eyes of a child.

Good News / Bad News

Again, I was thrilled to be included with such an exceptional cast. There were a few 'divas' in the mix, but they didn't bother me, I just thought they were silly. The tour started in September. Around January I started to feel tired. I noticed that it took extra effort to get through my song. I was sleepy all the time. Something was wrong with me. Could I be pregnant?

I took myself to a doctor in Los Angeles for a pregnancy test. The results were, "No. You are definitely not pregnant." Each passing day I felt worse and worse. I only had enough energy to do the show. No sight-seeing. No parties. Just the show. My imagination was starting to run wild with all of the possible diseases I might have.

When we got to Detroit, on my first day off, I went to a hospital clinic there. The internist said he would start a series of tests to determine why I felt so bad. He said that even though I'd just had a pregnancy test, he would have to show that he did one before he could administer some of the other tests. So I took another pregnancy test and was to return the following morning to start the other tests.

That evening, the doctor called me at the hotel. "I have good news and I have bad news. Which would you like first?" What a thing for a doctor to say, I thought to myself. "Well, give me the good news first." "You're not sick. You are definitely pregnant!" "So, what's the bad news?" I asked hesitantly. "We don't know how far along you are." While Tony stayed with Marie, I went back to the hospital clinic the next morning. It was determined that I was already about three months pregnant. Heavy doses of vitamins took care of the fatigue. The baby was due in September.

A few months after the tour started, the person who was in charge of the show souvenir merchandise on the road left the show. Jim came to me with the idea that perhaps Tony and I might be interested in taking over the merchandise. Tony would sell during the shows. Of course, that would mean that during the show, we'd have to have someone else watch Marie. He added that it could be quite lucrative for us.

I talked to Tony about the merchandise idea. We agreed to give it a try. We enjoyed being in the theater merchandise business and we were successful in finding terrific people to be with Marie during the show. Sometimes, if I felt uneasy about someone, I'd have the sitter and Marie come with me to the theater.

The show was due to open in New York just before the new baby was due. I suggested to Tony that we spend one of our weeks off in Hawaii. He wasn't sure we should go. He implied that it was a little "too extravagant." I told him to tell me where Marie and I should meet him when we got back. The three of us went to Hawaii. It was great fun.

During another break from the show we went back to New York to make arrangements with a doctor and decide on a hospital for the baby's birth. When it was determined that the baby was probably a girl, I decided to name her Julie. There was a wardrobe person on tour for a while whose name was Julie. She had such a warm and energetic personality that I always thought of sunshine when I saw her or said her name. To this day when I say "Julie" I think of sunshine.

In May, the show was in San Francisco. Every week the people who worked in wardrobe would let my costume out a little bit. However, I never did look pregnant. One night during the curtain call, I felt like I might faint. I told Tony I wanted him to take me to the hospital. The hospital he took me to was the same hospital where Marie had been born.

After my examination, one of the doctors told Tony and I that I was in labor. It was May. The baby wasn't due until September. One of the doctors spoke to us, "We can abort the baby now and you can continue with your tour. Or, you can try to bring the baby to term. That would mean bed rest for you for the rest of the pregnancy. The chances of the baby surviving don't look good." Funny how life works.

That night during the show, I had no idea that would be my last performance as Addaperle. I did not go to Japan or return to Broadway with *The Wiz*. I was admitted to San Francisco Children's Hospital. They did a procedure called a cervical cerclage. A cervical cerclage is the placement of stitches in the cervix to hold it closed to prevent miscarriage. I was placed in a bed and my feet were elevated far above my head to make sure the baby stayed in until September.

Needless to say I was depressed. I felt we'd made the right decision. I was happy about taking care of the new baby and doing everything I could to give her life. However, everything around me was happening so quickly. I missed the show. I missed my costume. I missed singing my song. I missed all the 'divas'. I missed Toto. I missed standing in the wings every night mesmerized each time Stephanie Mills sang *Home*. I missed my curtain call. I missed the magic.

I just now had a sinking feeling because I can't tell you what Marie was doing during all of this. For the life of me, I can't remember.

I'd been in the hospital on my head for almost a month when I was told I could go home. "Don't do too many steps and stay in bed as much as possible." Those were my orders from the doctor. Tony had rented us an apartment in the same vicinity of our last one. There was a long narrow set of stairs that led up to the apartment. After I'd been at my new home for about a week, Tony said I should at least go out with him for air. I reminded him of what the doctor said about stairs. Tony said he'd help me on the stairs, but he felt that being outside for just a little bit would make me feel better.

Against my better judgment, I went with him. Down the stairs and into the car. I don't remember exactly where we went. I do know that as soon as I got back in the car to go home, my waters broke and I went back to the hospital. This time the situation was critical. I was back on my head again. How much longer could they keep the baby in now that the waters had broken? They gave the baby steroids to develop her lungs while still inside of me.

The next morning it happened. Full-blown labor! The baby had to be born now. I was only six months into the pregnancy. I was wheeled into what looked like a small operating room. A female doctor tried to remove the cerclage. She wasn't able to do it as quickly as she wanted. Time was of the essence. I heard her yell "Emergency C!" Other medical staff members burst into the room. My only thought was that no one had put me to sleep. Do they know I'm still awake? "I'm not asleep!" I yelled. "Don't cut yet. I'm still awake. I'm still awake!"

"Mrs. Blondina, wake up." It was the gentle voice of that female doctor. Mrs. Blondina, your baby daughter has been born. Wake up now." When I opened my eyes I saw Tony and I saw the doctor. The baby was in intensive care. Later that day some doctors came to talk to Tony and me about Julie. "We're doing all we can for her, however, she will probably not live to see day seven."

Knowing that we had another daughter who was three, they encouraged us to bring Marie to see the new baby so that when we grieved and/or spoke of the baby she would have a better understanding of what was going on. I liked that idea. After day seven, they tried to prepare us for all of the physical and/or mental handicaps Julie was likely have.

Julie's whole body could fit in the palm of my hand and her tiny legs would dangle over the edge of my palm. She weighed a little over a pound. She had tubes connected everywhere and what looked like a patch over her left eye. I hated seeing her like that. When I first went home, I would come back to the hospital every day to spend time with Julie. And then, after the first month, I couldn't go any more. Tony continued to be there almost around the clock. On some days Marie went with him.

I couldn't go to the hospital. I couldn't go anywhere. I threw out my address book. I decided I was never going to call anyone again. I stopped answering my phone. I ignored any notes or letters that came from my theater friends. I wanted to do nothing. I didn't know what I was supposed to be thinking about. So, I just tried to sleep and think of nothing. My mother had flown from North Carolina to see about her new granddaughter. Family, friends and doctors were so concerned with the baby's health (as they should have been) that no one noticed I was not 'present' mentally. My mother took care of Marie during this time.

After three months in intensive care at San Francisco's Children's Hospital, she weighed in at three pounds. They told Tony and me to take her home. There was nothing else they could do. When the baby came home, I fell deeply in love with her. She was so tiny that we couldn't put blankets in her crib because she would get lost in the folds of the fabric. Marie was immediately a caring and protective sister. Today, we still refer to Julie as 'the miracle baby' because she beat the odds.

I Shop, Therefore I Am

The trauma and the drama surrounding Julie's birth left me emotionally devastated and mentally absent. While everyone was praying for the beautiful little miracle baby, no one noticed as mania consumed me. I didn't know why I felt so sad, or why I felt the need to separate myself from everyone. I didn't know why I was so angry. In retrospect, my life at this time was really wonderful. But it was as if I was blind to all that was good—all of the obvious miracles.

I didn't want to deal with other people. My world consisted of my children and my husband. I think Tony noticed there was something different emotionally going on with me. However, I think he just assumed it was because of all that had gone on with the baby and that I would soon start to act normal again.

I *did* know enough to know I didn't want Marie hanging out with a depressed mother all day. So, I enrolled her in a nursery school where she could play with other children and see happy people. I loved both of my children deeply. I loved taking care of them. I loved having them in my life. Yet, I was consumed with uncomfortable emotions I didn't know how to deal with. In fact, I was afraid to deal with them. I didn't want to think about them. I needed a diversion.

Shopping became my hobby. Shopping was something I could do alone or with my children. When I was shopping I wasn't thinking about my life. I wasn't feeling any pain or disappointment. I was looking at beautiful garments or jewelry or furniture. Shopping was my oxygen and I was gasping for life.

I would strap my babies in our new Honda and travel from Marin County across the Golden Gate Bridge into San Francisco to shop at the finest stores San Francisco had to offer. The sales associates at Neiman Marcus would fight over who was going to serve me. I remember arriving back home some days with my purchases and realizing I didn't have a matching belt for a particular outfit I had bought. Or perhaps, after arriving home, I noticed the color of a certain pair of earrings was off just a shade and didn't perfectly match the dress I intended to wear with it.

Well, I just strapped the children back in the car again. We would have to go back across the Golden Gate Bridge to San Francisco. I would not be able to sleep knowing that each and every outfit was not absolutely perfectly accessorized.

Tony started to comment about how much I was shopping. Once I got my purchases out of the bags and into the closet, he wouldn't really notice. So sometimes I would leave the bags in the car. And in the middle of the night I would go out, open up the bags, put the boxes and the bags and the paper in the outside garbage cans, and take my clothes inside and hang them in the closet as if they had been there all the time.

Part of my frustration was that I didn't feel he was proactive enough in finding work. He drove a taxi part time and worked for his father. I didn't trust his father. Sometimes when I would decide to do something without the children and Tony wasn't around, I would find different babysitters in my neighborhood to look after them until I returned. Tony's mother didn't understand why I would do this when she was at home and more than willing to spend time with her grandchildren.

Tony's mother was the kindest woman I ever met. I never heard her say an unkind word about anyone. She would be sad and disappointed if she found out I'd taken the girls to another sitter. The reason I didn't bring my children to her was because her husband would be there. I was not leaving my children with the man who stole my $20,000.

We used up my savings from the tour for living expenses and yes, my shopping. Before all the money dwindled away, I suggested we move back to New York where it was easier to find work in our particular fields of interest.

Dark and Then Dawn

When we first arrived back in New York we lived in Harlem in a basement apartment in a house owned by my sister's boyfriend. Tony and I were both trying to pull things together financially, but I guess it was too little too late. A few opportunities came my way but they involved traveling. I knew touring would never work with two children. The situation was getting bleak. Neither of us was working. I didn't want my children to suffer. I had to do something.

Without Tony's knowledge, I applied for public assistance. He was angry when he found out. However, the benefits couldn't have started at a more perfect time. Even he couldn't argue that as far as our children were concerned, this was a blessing. The interesting thing is that even though Tony never set foot in the welfare office and never filled out a single form, because we were married, they put all the benefits in *his* name.

Marie was five. Julie was three. I started to think about what schools they would attend. I wasn't familiar with the schools in Manhattan. So, I made it my business to try to check out all the pre-schools and elementary schools in the city so I could find the best ones, of course, for my children.

I saw some schools that were really nice. I saw some schools that I couldn't believe were operating as schools, and that parents actually let their children go there. I started looking at private schools too. I just threw caution to the wind and didn't look or worry about price. I just decided I wanted to see what was out there—what the possibilities were.

Of course, some schools I attempted to visit wouldn't even let me in. Others let me in but were extremely unpleasant to me. I assumed this was because they assumed I couldn't afford their school. They were right. I couldn't afford their schools. However, it sometimes felt like that old Jim Crow law or segregation feeling coming back where I was treated like a second-class citizen as a child. I hated being broke. But couldn't I dream? Besides, all that had to happen for us to be back on our feet again was for me to be cast in a long-running hit on Broadway or a popular TV commercial.

There was one school that I saw on New York's upper West Side that I fell in love with. It was a private school and they *did* let me come in. The people were friendly and I was able to look around and talk to the teachers. I loved this school! The atmosphere was upbeat. The staff seemed positive. The children were respected. I felt this was the place I wanted my children to be. The kids there seemed so happy and there was such peacefulness about the place.

I inquired about how much the school would cost. It wasn't exorbitant like some of the others. It was pretty affordable. But affordability is always relative. So, even though it was only about $600 a month per child, it might as well have been $6,000.

I'd befriended a woman who lived across the street from me who lived in a large housing project. I would see her in the mornings when she was taking her son to school. She's the one who told me about this school that I'd fallen in love with. It took me a few days to get up the courage to ask, because I felt it may have been an invasive question. But the next time I saw her, without hesitating, I just said, "How can you afford to send your son to the school you told me about?"

She said, "Oh, just go back and tell them that you want to be on *the plan*."

Well, I didn't even ask her what that meant, but I do know that the next day, bright and early, I went back to the school, walked up to the receptionist and said, "I'm interested in my children attending your school. I love your school and I want them to be on *the plan*."

Now mind you, I still had no idea what the plan was, if I was saying it correctly, or if this woman was just pulling something out of the air. But immediately the woman behind the desk gave me some forms and she said, "We'll need proof of income. How many children are we talking about?"

"Two." She gave me more forms.

"We'd like to meet your children. Can you come back to tomorrow with proof of income and bring your children with you?"

When we arrived at West Side Montessori the next day, Marie and Julie immediately felt comfortable and seemed happy there. I was happy for them. The teachers and administrators at the school went out of their way to talk to us and make us feel comfortable.

A few days later I received a phone call from the school. Marie and Julie were accepted into the school on *the plan*. The school accepted a certain amount of students whose families couldn't afford the school in an effort to insure diversity in the school. Or, at least this was my understanding of *the plan*. My fee was based on a sliding scale. I was to pay according to my income. I thought, "Now that's a really good plan. Thank you God!"

A few months later I got a job at Saks Fifth Avenue as a sales associate. I knew all of their merchandise and this type of environment extremely well. All of that California shopping left me with knowledge of designers, store merchandise and procedures. I had great customer service skills because I knew what I expected and desired during my many shopping experiences.

In a short time I had a clientele that trusted me to shop for them. They didn't even bother coming into the store. They'd call me at the store and tell me an ideal designer, a size and an ideal color. I would shop for them and have their packages sent to their homes. It was a fancy store with a lot of well-to-do patrons. However, the pay was not so fancy. Tony was driving taxis part time. Financially, we were still struggling.

My sister's boyfriend turned out to be a pathological liar who was living a double life. When my sister broke up with him, he immediately tried to evict me, Tony and our daughters from his apartment we were renting. He created false allegations and took us to housing court. We were able to prove in court that all of his charges were false. However, I no longer felt safe renting from him. Tony felt we could work something out with him. I started looking for apartments.

The apartments in Manhattan that we could afford, I either didn't feel safe in, or they were way too small for the four of us. I don't remember how I ended up in Brooklyn, but I found a beautiful, large, newly renovated loft apartment near Coney Island. My mother gave us money for the upfront fees for the Brooklyn loft. We moved to Brooklyn. It felt good.

Our loft was the top floor over some storefront businesses. By six o'clock each day, the businesses would close. We were the only tenants there at night. Marie and Julie could play and be as loud as they wanted. We also had access to the roof where we would sit in the evenings and just look at the stars.

At about the same time, Tony started working managing various Broadway show's merchandise and souvenirs like we had done on *The Wiz* tour. Eric Krebs, a producer and theater manager offered me a job as general manager of the John Houseman Theater Complex. He controlled the complex at that time. I'd met Eric when I was cast in a production of a show called *Little Ham* that he produced one summer at Westport Country Playhouse in Connecticut.

I didn't know a lot about managing a theatre complex at that time. However, he said he hired me because I was the only person he could stand to work around for long periods of time. I had no difficulty getting along with Eric, and even though I wasn't onstage, it was theater. I quit my job at Saks Fifth Avenue to take the general manager's job. I loved my new job.

Getting my children up in the mornings, feeding and dressing them, taking the D train from Brooklyn to Manhattan, switching to the #1 train to 96th Street, walking the two blocks to their school, hugging, kissing, saying goodbye, catching the #1 train back downtown and switching to the A train to the Times Square stop, and then walking three really long blocks to my job felt like a day's work in itself. Not to mention working at the theater and then rushing to make sure I picked my children up on time from the school, and then traveling back to Brooklyn with them.

In the evenings there was dinner to prepare, baths, playtime and a little bit of house cleaning. When I recall that period of time, I get exhausted just thinking about it. Tony was working in the evenings and was usually gone by the time we got home. He played with Marie and Julie when he was home, but I carried the brunt of the child-raising and household responsibilities. However, God sent me an angel.

I cannot remember how I asked or what I asked, or whom I asked, but somehow I must have gotten the word out that I was looking for somebody to help me. God sent me Louise, a beautiful, energetic Haitian woman who loved life and caring for and sharing with others. She was wonderful! She lived near me in Brooklyn. I wasn't able to pay her very much. But she agreed to work for me. Her job was to pick up my children at our apartment in Brooklyn, take them to school, and pick them up in the evenings and bring them back.

However, Louise would show up early in the morning, cook my children breakfast, get them dressed and take them to school, come back to the apartment, clean up, wash dishes, and then pick up my kids from school, bring them home and entertain them until I got there. Marie and Julie loved Louise. I was so happy she was a part of our lives.

I Lost That Lovin' Feelin'

It almost seems like it happened overnight; I no longer felt supported or truly loved by Tony. It felt as if we were living in two different worlds. We seldom agreed on anything. His money was his money. He would say I could have anything I wanted if I could make the money to pay for it. Those old days in the dressing rooms, when Tony made me feel so good—I felt happy just sitting next to him—when we made each other laugh out loud, were now dim memories.

For instance, even though I worked at the theater complex during the day and he mostly worked in the evenings, if ever there was a call from the school, or one of the children needed to go to the doctor, he assumed I would leave my job to take care of it, even if he was not working during those hours.

I also had an opportunity to do a show called *Nunsense* in a town near Albany. Eric agreed I could take the time off to do the show. It was such a fun and silly show. I'd always wanted to play the role of Sister Mary Hubert. I was so-o-o excited. However, I didn't get any help or support from my husband for this project. He felt it didn't pay enough. So, I was on my own. Looking back I don't know how I did it. However, I'm sure it involved Louise and my sister's help. I managed to get through rehearsals and got great reviews for my performance in the show. The show was at a venue called The Cohoes Music Hall in Cohoes, NY. Marie and Julie came with me on several occasions.

This may seem silly, but I wanted my little girls to have pretty dresses and "dress-up" shoes. He felt it was okay for them just to have sneakers and pants, and felt I was wasting money when I bought these things for my daughters.

He'd never bought me an engagement or wedding ring. I started bringing that up whenever we had disagreements. One day, when he was tired of hearing about the ring, he insisted that I go with him to a jewelry store to make sure the fit was right. The ring was beautiful and I told him so, but what I didn't tell him was I didn't want it. I felt like he only got the ring so I would shut up about it, not because he really wanted to buy me a ring.

However, the straw that broke the camel's back was when I told him that the girls needed beds. Up till now, they had been sleeping on padded mattresses on the floor. He did not think that purchasing beds was necessary. A theater friend bought my children bunk beds and I bought the mattresses.

Anger and depression took turns visiting me. I was really good at hiding them. I became a master at putting on a cheerful facade. I started going to a clinic for psychiatric counseling. I was immediately put on

Elavil—an antidepressant. At first, I felt dizzy and less energetic from the medication. But I stuck with it. I didn't know what else to do. My therapist said, "Your body just needs to get used to it." I needed for this medication to make me feel better. I kept taking it. Although it didn't make me feel better, I kept thinking, "I just have to stick with it. I know it's going to work. It has to."

Sometimes on my way to work from Brooklyn to Times Square, I couldn't remember which subway I should take. And, when I was on a subway, I couldn't always remember the stop where I needed to get off. It was as if my brain would shut down. I wondered how much longer I'd be able to pretend I was fine. More and more I would arrive at work and sit in my office and just move papers around on my desk for hours.

I was happy with my job at the theater. I loved the responsibility. I loved learning new things every day. I loved interacting with the producers and actors who would come through to rent rehearsal space. Louise was still a great help.

However, I eventually started to feel disconnected. I didn't feel like I was a part of the real world. Something was missing. I wanted my old husband and the times when we used to laugh and talk for hours. I wanted the Tony I felt safe with and who'd encouraged me to dream seemingly impossible dreams. I could not find him and eventually, I stopped looking for him. I wanted a divorce.

Years earlier, when I was doing *Godspell* in Washington, DC, one of my neighbors used to invite me to listen to tapes with her of a preacher named Reverend Ike. I remembered that listening to those tapes made me feel good. It suddenly dawned on me that I was in New York City so I could go see Reverend Ike in person every Sunday.

And, that's just what I started doing. On Sundays I would dress my girls and we would take the A Train uptown to The Palace Cathedral at Broadway and 175th Street. The sermons comforted me. Most of the time, my children would stay upstairs with Miss Mary. Miss Mary was a kindhearted woman who cared for children whose parents were attending the services. The children got lots of love, cookies and fruit juice while they were there. My daughters were quite fond of Miss Mary. I would be downstairs being mesmerized by one of Reverend Ike's sermons. I looked forward to the times when he would lead the congregation in a song called *I Got the Power.*

Rev. Ike (Frederick Eikerenkoetter) was a controversial minister because he was wealthy and proud of his wealth. He loved to talk about his Rolls-Royces. Many people were uncomfortable with a minister who had as much money as he did. However, the majority of people were even more uncomfortable with him because of his flamboyant preaching style and messages that went against the grain of most religious messages.

The church was called the Palace Cathedral and was ornately decorated with gold filigree. He interpreted the Bible "psychologically, rather than theologically," to teach us positive self-awareness. Despite what people may have thought of him, I loved hearing him talk about the "Power of God" within me.

His teachings were a lot different from what I remember hearing about Jesus and God when I was growing up in Greensboro. Among other things, he preached, "Everything is a condition of the mind." What is interesting is, even though I didn't understand exactly what he was talking about, it felt good to hear it.

However, the more I got involved in the church, I realized even though I loved the message, I didn't like being part of an organization. With everything that was going on in my life, members of the church were encouraging me to take on more responsibilities and show up for more programs and meetings. I didn't have the energy. Over time I became caught up in my day to day life challenges. I started focusing on all that was wrong in my life, to the point that I forgot about how good Reverend Ike's sermons made me feel. I started to see getting my children dressed and traveling there on Sundays as a chore.

I managed to isolate myself from other people. I was soon living in my own little world that consisted of one problem after another. I was sad. I was angry. I was scared. I was tired. I was confused. Nothing made sense to me. It was not uncommon for me to break things like my cassette recorder, a record album, or a dish by smashing them on the floor out of sheer frustration. However, I was able to put on an emotional and physical facade that was amazing. I dressed neat and tidy. Makeup flawless. I still managed a bright smile for the public. And, I'd not lost my ability to provide comic relief when a public situation called for it.

They Are Trying To Get Me

I moved me and my daughters out of the Brooklyn loft. Through one of my sister's clients, I found a two-bedroom apartment in Harlem near where we used to live. Our new apartment was the third floor of a brownstone. I was officially separated from Tony.

I don't remember what he said or what I said. I wanted to be away—on my own. Louise helped us moved and wished us well. We promised to stay in touch. Getting the children to and from school was a lot easier now that I was back in Manhattan. Our new apartment was a short train ride away from their school, and even a taxi back and forth on rainy days was affordable now.

Tony's day off was usually Monday. He would come and get Marie and Julie on Sunday evenings after his last show and take them to the Brooklyn loft. He would also take them to school on Mondays and Tuesdays. I would pick them up on Tuesday after school and they would be with me until Sunday again.

Mentally and physically I was not doing well. I was exhausted. I loved my children more than anything and did my best to take care of them. They were my allies. It was me and them against the world. I had fun with them I enjoyed playing with them and being silly with them. I would sing compositions of my own, collectively known as "The Underwear Songs," in the morning.

It was a different song each day. I sang it as if it were a big Broadway show number. It would be a song about the color underwear each child was going to wear that day, or a song about the designs on it, and then I would add verses about the joys and trials of trying to get dressed in the mornings. Then the days came when the children would say, "Mommy sing The Underwear Song." I would look and sigh. "Not today. Perhaps, tomorrow." I just wanted to lie down.

At work, I started to believe that *they* were trying to *get me*. Someone there was trying to *get me*. Perhaps it was Eric. It could have been one of any number of people who rented offices and space in that building. I had to get out. I had to leave. I could no longer work under these conditions. I asked myself, "Why were *they* trying to *get me*?"

Of course, no one was trying to get me. I was being totally paranoid. But at that time, it seemed real. I told Eric I needed to leave. To this day, I'm not exactly sure what he must have been thinking when I told him that. He had a one-man show opening on Broadway. The charismatic actor, Avery Brooks, was playing Paul Robeson in a show of the same title. Eric told me Mr. Brooks needed an assistant during the show and offered me that job. I suppose, I assume Eric thought it would be less stressful. Obviously, in retrospect, Eric did not see me as a woman who was having a total meltdown.

However, I think he soon got that message. I started working with Mr. Brooks. And frankly, it was a dream job. Imagine, my job was to assist this wonderful, beautiful, gorgeous, handsome, talented, tall, fabulous black man who was starring in this magnificent Broadway show. Part of my duties involved helping him get his costume buttoned up. Many women would have killed for this job. But because I was living in a world in my head that was a nightmare, I could not see this as a dream job.

I was always kind and courteous to Mr. Brooks. I made sure he had everything he needed to have a successful show, and this included making sure his tuxedos and tuxedo shirts were clean and in good repair for each show. I was the one responsible for washing and ironing the shirts.

Okay. Are you sitting down? About a week into the show, I went to Eric and I said, "I will not do this job. You think because I am black that I'm supposed to wash and iron people's clothes. Well, I will not do it." I quit that job.

There was nobody I could trust. There was no one who understood me. I did not understand me. My children deserved a better mother than me. Life was too hard. I wanted out. There had to be a way out of this life.

They Wanted My Bed

I started to believe the little green and black capsules the doctor at the clinic had prescribed were not going to work. I liked the woman who was my therapist. However, I was tired of talking to her and seeing no results. I wanted to be well. I wanted to be normal. I felt more tired and frustrated every day. Marie and Julie made me happy. Yet, I felt they deserved a mother who wasn't crazy, and a mother who could provide better for them financially.

It was only about a week after I quit working for Eric and the Paul Robeson show that I decided I could no longer go on like this. So, one morning after my daughters were at school, I decided this would be the day that I got out. I took the # 1 train to Broadway and 125th Street. I got out at that station because at that station the tracks are high up off the ground. I thought perhaps I would jump from those tracks.

And the more I contemplated that jump; I thought there must be somebody in this city that could help me. By now tears were streaming down my face. I couldn't stop crying. I took the train down to a midtown hospital. I approached a desk where two ladies were sitting. I couldn't stop crying so I couldn't speak. I just stood there crying. They started to laugh. One said to the other, "So, this fool just going to stand here and cry."

The more I cried, the more they laughed. I felt totally humiliated and saw this as confirmation that I just needed to go somewhere and die.

I hastily turned and rushed out the door. I wasn't looking where I was going and I was blinded by my tears and I bumped into a woman. I apologized, but she grabbed me by my arm as I was walking away. She asked, "Why are you crying?" But I could only cry. She took me by the arm and brought me back to the hospital with her.

She brought me into a room and offered me water and stayed with me until I was able to talk. I don't remember what I said when I finally did talk. It turns out she was a psychiatrist who practiced at that hospital. She gave me a pill that she said would help calm me down. She wanted my sister's phone number because I told her that she was my closest relative. I don't know if I mentioned Tony or not. She wanted to know where my children were. The next thing I remember is waking up the next day in a hospital bed. I had been admitted to the psychiatric unit at St. Luke-Roosevelt Hospital. I was exhausted. All I wanted to do was sleep.

The doctor insisted that I speak to my children and let them know they were not the reason why I was in the hospital—it was not their fault. I was happy she suggested that. I spoke to them over the phone while she watched on. And then, I went back to sleep. Roberta took over my bills. Roberta, Louise and Tony took care of Marie and Julie.

I was in that hospital for nearly a month. I started to feel comfortable there. I remember wishing that perhaps I could just live there. For nearly three weeks all I did was eat a little and sleep a lot. I could not get enough sleep. I'm sure some of the medication I was taking contributed to this drowsy feeling. However, sleep is the most wonderful "life escape" I know.

After the first few weeks in the hospital, they asked me to participate in some of the patient activities. I didn't want to. I just wanted to sit and do nothing. But the staff kept stressing how important it was that I participate in the activities. I finally agreed to go to arts and crafts one day. I made a trivet (a stand used under a hot dish on a table) using colored stones that I glued to a piece of metal.

The woman psychiatrist who'd admitted me to the hospital was kind and patient with me. However, she told me I needed to start preparing to leave the hospital. "I suppose I could leave now," I thought to myself, "But I'm too afraid. There's no way I'm leaving now," I thought. Well, as my mother used to say, "God works in mysterious ways."

Just a few days later, people were checking in in droves. I remember seeing gurneys with people on them lined up along the hallways. There were people moaning and crying and some just not saying anything. Where were all these people coming from? The psychiatrist who had been so wonderful to me while I was in the hospital came and spoke to me.

I'm not sure of her exact words right now. However, the meaning was this: since we believe you're able to cope on the outside a little better than these people who are waiting to be admitted, we're going to discharge you because there are a lot of people who need to come in here and we need your bed.

It was October 19th 1987. I would later find out that the largest one day stock market crash in history happened on this day. Within one day, 500 billion dollars evaporated from the Dow Jones index. Many people lost millions instantly. According to news reports, some unstable individuals, who had lost fortunes, went to their broker's offices and started shooting.

Hundreds of people fell into deep depressions or were suicidal, and they wanted my bed. Isn't life interesting? *They* wanted my bed. Many of these people who, only hours before, would have probably had nothing to do with the mentally ill. I'm sure some of these people would have laughed at me that day when I couldn't stop crying. I imagined that many of them, 24 hours earlier, would have said that I, and people like me, just needed to work harder and pull ourselves up by our boot straps. "Stop whining and wasting our tax dollars." However, now, *they* wanted—they needed my bed. Suddenly, I was an outpatient.

The psychiatrist took me on as a private patient. When we both noticed how quickly I was gaining weight from the antidepressants, she and I were both concerned. She told me about a brand new medication that might help control the weight gain. I went from a size 4 to a size 8 in only a few months. The medication I'd been given in the hospital was replaced with something called Prozac. Prozac did stop the weight gain and I actually liked it. I didn't notice any side-effects and I had more energy than I did on most of the other medications. I felt drugged, but I didn't feel like a zombie.

Within a few weeks, I was feeling better. I was still a little weak physically, and embarrassed a lot. My children came back to live with me in my Harlem apartment. Within about a month, it was almost as if I'd never been away. My life was about getting Marie and Julie to and from school and trying to keep the bills paid. Tony was still living in the apartment in Brooklyn. We started the old routine of the children spending Sunday night through Tuesday with their father.

My daughters and I started watching a local cable TV show called *First Exposure*. The show was broadcasted live from a small studio in the Bronx on Friday evenings. *First Exposure* allowed rappers, singers, spokes models, and other local performers to showcase their talent. It was a low budget show, but some of the talent was extraordinary, and it looked like they were having a lot of fun.

I contacted the producer and was given a slot on one of the shows. The performers would lip-sink to a song they had previously recorded. I performed one of the songs from the demo tape I'd done in San Francisco when I was calling myself "The African Violet." I was excited and wanted everything to be just right. You would have thought I was gong to be on the Johnny Carson Show. My sister bought me a black cocktail dress from Macy's. I braided a lot of long wavy extensions in my hair. It was the most fun I'd had in a while. I was invited back two more times.

I didn't have anyone to look after Marie and Julie after the first show. But I enjoyed it so much I wanted to go back, so I took them with me. The stage was set up informally with guests and other artists sitting around the perimeter of the stage in the background. Marie and Julie could be seen in a couple of shows when they aired.

At about the same time, I also wanted to perform with the Apollo Theater house band. This was a few years before the shows were televised. I knew that the Apollo audience could be ruthless, but I was willing to take that chance. I wanted to sing on *that* stage. That night I performed a Millie Jackson arrangement of a song called *The Angel In Your Arms* originally recorded by Hot, then by Reba McIntyre.

I was good. It also felt good to be on that stage belting out my song. I got through the whole song and the clown didn't come out to sweep me away. If a contestant was performing badly or the audience booed a lot, it was customary for a clown to dance on stage and sweep the performer off.

A white girl from Queens won that night. She *was* a good singer. However, I like to think it's because she had three bus loads of supporters with her. So at the end, they clapped and screamed much louder for her than the rest of the audience did for me. Marie and Julie were in the audience that night too.

Financially I was in a crunch; Tony took care of the children when they were with him, but when they were with me I was on my own. I went to the welfare office early one Tuesday morning. I'd gone the day before, however, I didn't realize you had to show up ridiculously early—before the office opened—to get a number to insure you would be seen by someone.

Tuesday was a good morning because the children would have been with Tony over the weekend and he would take them to school on Monday and Tuesday morning. I was in line at the welfare office at 6:30 a.m. When the office opened, each person in line was given a number according to their position in line. I was number twenty-three.

All day I sat there and waited to hear my number called. I didn't eat. I didn't drink. I don't remember if I even went to the bathroom. I sat and waited to hear number 23. I watched the clock and as it got closer to 2:30 p.m. I started to panic a little bit. I thought for sure I would be out by 2:30. I had not made arrangements for anyone to pick Marie up from school. I had until 6:00 p.m. to pick Julie up.

However, Marie, who was now in first grade at Saint John Divine Cathedral School, would be out of school at 2:30. I flew out of the office at about 2:15 and jumped on the A Train down to 110th Street. Ran every step of the way to my daughter's school, grabbed her and ran back to the train, back to 125th Street, and ran as fast as we could back to the welfare office. When I approached the receptionist's desk I was so out of breath I could hardly talk. "I'm number 23."

"And you're telling me this because . . .?" The receptionist acted as if she really didn't know why I was telling her this. So, I realized I was going to have to play this game with her.

"I'm telling you this because when I got here this morning at 6:30, I was given number 23. At 2:30 I had to pick my daughter up from school. I'm back now. I'm number 23."

"We skipped your number. You weren't here when it was called."

"I had to get my daughter from school. I'm back now. I am number 23."

"You will have to come back and get a new number tomorrow morning. We skipped your number. We don't go backwards."

Without thinking, I pushed everything off her desk. I then went around to various desks lifting them so that everything would slide off the desk or pushing things off with my hands. I was suddenly blinded by what seemed like all the pent up anger, rage, frustration, fear and hurt from this lifetime and any lifetime before. I ripped all of the posters off the walls. Posters that said: "Know your rights", "Are you eligible for food stamps?", "How do you know if you have HIV?", and "No education equals no future."

When I stopped, tears were rolling down my face. One of my hands was bleeding. My daughter was crying. My mind was blank and I had no energy to move. I heard someone say," Call the police!" Within seconds, six policemen were coming toward me. I was unable to talk. Marie was trying to explain about the number 23.

There was one black cop who seemed more aggressive than the others. He just kept saying to the other policemen, "I got this. I got this." I heard him tell the other policemen in a real sinister voice, "Oh please, let me handle this one." He was almost laughing. He pushed the other cops aside and escorted me and my daughter out of the building. The people who worked at the welfare office were asking each other if they were all right. Some were yelling, "Arrest her! Put her in jail! Put her under the jail!" And the policeman, who had me by the arm and my daughter by the hand yelled back, "You got it!"

I was sure I was going to be thrown in jail. And I'd probably never see my daughter again. Oh god! What had I done? Oh god! What had I done now? By now my daughter was hysterical. I didn't know how to comfort her. While some of the people from the welfare office were watching, he ordered me to get into the back seat of his police car. I held on to my daughters hand as tight as I could. We drove about three blocks away, out of sight and around the corner from the welfare office.

The officer pulled the car over, turned to my daughter and said in the gentlest voice I could imagine any police officer ever speaking in, "Don't cry little girl. I'm not going to take your mama to jail. Is your mama sick? Has she ever been in the hospital?" I heard Marie answer yes. Then he turned to me, "Did you eat anything today? Did you take your medication today?" I managed to get out a very weak, "No."

He asked my daughter where we lived and he drove us to the brownstone where we lived. Before we got out of the car, he told Marie that I was not feeling well and that she should call somebody to come and help me. He asked Marie, "So, who are you going to call?"

She said, "Aunt Roberta." We got out of his car and he watched us go in before driving away. Marie called my sister. I don't know what Marie told her, but my sister picked Julie up from school that evening and brought her home. I don't remember what else happened that night. I don't know who that policeman was or where he is today. I do know he was an angel, I often think about him. I love him.

Bags Of Money

As things around me started settling back down to I guess what we would call normal, or what was passing for normal, a social worker from my doctor's office helped get the welfare claim through. We lived on welfare and food stamps for about 4 months. During that time, we learned what I refer to as shopping for cash.

You see, the food stamps we received only bought food items. If you bought something at the store with a food stamp, you would receive change back in food stamps, unless the change was under $1. Sometimes, however, we'd have plenty of food stamps but no toilet tissue or toothpaste or laundry detergent or bus or subway fare or extra money for a school trip.

So, I came up with a legal way to get the cash out of the food stamps. Each of us would take turns going into a grocery store that had 25 cent bags of potato or corn chips. The idea was to buy only one bag at a time. We would pay with a food stamp. No matter the denomination of the stamp, we'd always get at least 75 cents back in change. We'd do this enough times in enough stores until we had enough change to buy the items we needed cash for.

I was still going to therapy and taking Prozac and other prescription drugs for depression or anxiety from time to time. At the suggestion of my doctor, Marie and Julie had their own therapists that they saw regularly as well. They were still spending weekends with Tony. I decided to communicate with him as little as possible. Our discussions usually ended with some type of disagreement. However; in general, I was feeling happy and was starting to have a positive outlook about the future.

My sister hired me to work in her office full time. I even enrolled in a millinery class at the Harlem Institute of Fashion. I quickly learned how to design and create all kinds of hats from scratch. I loved it. I now know that making hats became my meditation, allowing me to leave this world without destroying the body. I could lose myself in hat making and designing for hours at a time. When I was making hats I was no longer in this 3-D world or bothered by any of life's challenges.

Little by little I acquired wooden blocks for blocking my hats, and all of the necessary equipment to make any kind of hat anyone could possibly want. My apartment walls were covered with all kinds of amazing and colorful hats. I wore a different hat every day. Sometimes, I couldn't sleep at night because I'd have an idea for a hat and I'd have to get up and make it. Every bead, rock, string, piece of fabric, feather, silk flower, dried flower, rhinestone or old broach was, to me, an idea and a reason to make a new hat.

One day, JoJo, my childhood friend who now lived in Harlem too, came by to check on me and my daughters. When he walked in and saw all the hats on the walls, he gasped. He then looked at me and said, "I don't believe you! You claim you never have enough money. Look at these walls. This is a gold mine. Start selling this stuff!"

I started doing a few street festivals and special events around Harlem. Before long I expanded my line to include jewelry and other accessories—all made by my very own hands. I was having a good time. Was I making a lot of money? No. But, I loved every minute of it. I was interacting with people, I was creative. My children were excited and enjoyed setting up the displays and helping potential buyers. I was happy.

A couple of months after I'd been working for my sister, I had to take one of the children to the doctor. I was surprised when the clinic told me I would have to pay because my children no longer had Medicaid.

I thought this was odd because I understood once a parent started working and gave up public assistance her children were still covered for a period of time, and that time had not passed yet. I asked a Legal Aid assistant about this and she agreed with me and advised me to appeal the decision.

So I did appeal. On three occasions, early in the morning, I went to an appointment at a court building in lower Manhattan. The person who was assigned as my legal counsel or advocate would meet me there each time. The first two times, the representative from the State of New York State never showed up. However, on the third occasion when a representative from the state failed to showed up for the appointment, the judge started banging his gavel and saying some things that I didn't understand. I first thought the judge was angry with me for some reason. My advocate leaned over to me and asked if I understood what was happening. I said, "No."

She said, "The judge is angry and tired of the state representatives not showing. He is not only granting your children Medicaid. He is also taking your case back (I forget how many months) and demanding that the state pay you public assistance and food stamps at the rate and amount that you were receiving prior to going back to work."

At first I didn't know how to feel. It was like hitting the lottery. But, I didn't want to get too happy because I thought it was just the judge grandstanding and nobody was really going to give me that amount of money.

However, about a week later I received a notice in the mail that I could take my old public assistance card, go to a qualified check cashing place (that's how it used to be done in New York City) and get the cash and the food stamps. I was advised to take someone with me because it would be a lot of cash. It was so much money that the computer was not able to dispense it all in one day. I had to go back the next day to get the rest of the cash and the food stamps. I literally had a shopping bag full of food stamps and a shopping bag full of cash.

This was me and my children's ticket out of New York City. It looked like we were going to remain poor, and I did not want to be poor in New York City. I paid my dear friend, the late Luther Fontaine, a talented Broadway actor and dancer, to rent a truck and drive our belongings to North Carolina. My children and I had gone ahead of him by bus. To this day, I honestly don't know what I said to Tony about the move, or if I even said anything at all.

If you were ever to look up the words "outstanding friend", you would find Luther Fontaine's picture. When I think back on those times now, I don't know how he put up with me. I was always in some crisis or another. I would call him to bitch and complain. He would tell me why I was justified or unjustified in being angry. I would call him when I was scared. I also called him when I was happy. He always took my calls. I don't know if he would just lay the receiver down and walk away until I was finished venting or not. However, I do know that he never hung up on me. Even *I* would have hung up on me.

I originally met him when I was working as general manager of the Houseman Theater Complex. We realized we had done many of the same shows and had worked with many of the same people. Luther taught at the La Rocque Bey School of Dance located at the Harlem YMCA, so I enrolled Marie and Julie. On Saturday mornings they took African dance with La Rocque Bey and tap dance classes from Luther.

Right Back Where I Started

The summer of 1989, I arrived back in North Carolina excited about starting a new life. At the same time I was embarrassed about my mental health history and mental hospital admissions. I felt like I'd failed. I wanted to entertain people. I wanted to be on Broadway again and do tours of fabulous shows and put on make-up and sign autographs. I'd thought I would travel the world. Instead, I was waiting in welfare lines and was in and out of mental hospitals. I was right back were I started from. I felt too embarrassed to want to see old friends. So, I didn't. I didn't visit. I didn't return calls. My life was about taking care of my children.

The money from the welfare settlement allowed me to rent a nice two-bedroom apartment in a decent neighborhood. Of course, it was possible to live well in North Carolina for a lot less than it would cost to live the same lifestyle in New York. Getting around in Greensboro without a car was extremely difficult. I was going to need a car. My mother had been looking for a way to justify getting a newer car. She graciously gave me her immaculate red 1978 Chevrolet Nova.

Marie was going into the second grade and Julie was going to be in kindergarten. My mother seemed happy that we were in North Carolina and seemed eager to help us in any way she could. She had recently retired as a nurse's aid from the L. Richardson Hospital. My mother and I had different ideas about how to raise children so we clashed a lot.

For instance, I didn't then, and I still don't believe in spanking or hitting children for any reason unless it's in self-defense. I believe in disciplining children, but I don't believe that discipline equals hitting. Many people tell me that you have to spank your kids to keep them in line. I believe just the opposite is true.

I believe we need to hug our kids more, talk to our children more, and honor our children more. But, I know I'm in the minority in my thinking. Therefore, I have just resolved to agree to disagree with everyone else's view about hitting children. My mother is one of those who believed that every now and then you need to "tear that little behind up."

We also disagreed on the types of foods my daughters should eat. It was harder for me to control this aspect because I was not there to police them when my mother was taking care of them. So she usually got away with feeding them what she wanted to feed them no matter what I said on the subject. My ideas about what was healthy food had changed since I was a child. Also, my mother was using more packaged food than we used when I was a child.

My mother believed that using the new packaged, timesaving foods was a way of being part of the new, modern world. Despite our different views on child rearing, it felt good to be back where my mother was. Somehow during the years growing up, things seem so rushed. I was looking forward to experiencing my mother and loving my mother, and having my mother experience and love me for who I was now.

I was determined to work and find ways to make a lot of money. I was still designing hats and accessories but I had no knowledge of how to market them. I could probably figure that out but in the meantime, I wanted cash coming in immediately.

I took the first job I was offered—cashier at Burger King. I was told my job was to serve the customers and ring up their sales. I found it fun. I enjoyed interacting with the customers and I especially liked using the register with icons of the products on it. I felt more like I was playing than working. This job lasted 2 days because on the second day, a new young manager told me that my job duties also included cleaning the bathrooms every day, and mopping down the kitchen every other day. This was not in the original job description. I was not that desperate for money yet. I still had lots of money and food stamps in the shopping bags in my closet. I'd keep looking.

My other jobs included telephone survey person, department store make-up artist (I'd studied make-up artistry during my early years in New York and had a certificate from a well respected make-up school), fashion show coordinator, home water purification system salesperson (left when I found out the company was scamming their clients), working in the mall getting people to sign up for various store credit cards.

I was still struggling with depression and fatigue. However, most of the jobs ended because they were only temporary. Finding a job that paid a decent wage was not as easy as I thought it would be. I found myself in a catch-22. I wasn't making money so I was more depressed, but because I was more depressed I couldn't focus on how to make money. After a year at the nice apartment, the money was starting to dwindle, and I wasn't able to work hard enough or fast enough to keep my children and me from sinking. I was not shopping like before. In fact, I was being very careful and responsible with the money. I was frustrated and angry because I didn't know how to provide for us—I didn't know how to make us rich. We were still struggling. The day came when I could no longer pay the rent on the nice apartment.

I soon found myself applying for public housing. Public housing rent was based on your income. When I moved into the public housing community my rent was $0.00 a month. My mother, who was on a fixed income herself, thought this was appalling. My mother was living on her social security retirement

payments and whatever benefits my father had ac-
cumulated when he worked at the post office. She
had always applauded herself for never needing any
type of public assistance. She went to the housing
community office one day and insisted on giving them
something toward my rent. Of course, that is not how
it worked and they couldn't take her money.

I Killed A Boy

The public housing community we moved to consisted of about 50 units. We lived in a small two-story, two-bedroom apartment which was attached to two other units. Downstairs, there was a kitchen and living room, and upstairs were two bedrooms and a bathroom. The apartment was sparsely furnished with decent pieces I'd taken with me from New York. I had the basics: a bed for each of us, a sofa, a TV, VCR player, stereo system, plates, dishes, cookware and a few African fabric prints and inexpensively framed art prints on the wall.

Also, my mother made sure my daughters and I had what we needed to live as she would say, "a presentable" life. Actually, the apartments were pretty nice compared to apartments I had lived in in New York. This apartment in New York City would go for at least $2,000 a month."

The only thing that ever struck me as really odd about this apartment was how the front door and the front of the buildings and large porches faced in toward a courtyard. The back door and back yard of the buildings faced the street. This meant that when people drove by they were actually seeing the back of our houses where we put the mops to dry, and kitchen windows etc. No one ever saw the front of our homes which looked much nicer.

When we moved to public housing it was kind of intimidating for us. Even though we'd lived in New York, we'd led a more sheltered life. Some of the children—and adults I met loved to argue and thought fighting was the best way to settle a dispute. Because my children's father is white and I'm black, my children looked neither white nor black, and the children at their school and in our public housing neighborhood weren't sure how to categorize them.

They weren't sure what I was either, because in those days, I was wearing my hair in dreadlocks or Nubian locks. Locks or dreads were not popular then. So the kids would call me 'African' as if that were supposed to be an insult. The adults were not that much better. Because I had locks, even strangers thought it was okay to tell me to "Comb your hair girl!" It makes me smile when I see that many of the people who wanted me to comb my hair are now wearing dread locks or Nubian locks or some kind of lock themselves today, now that it's considered fashionable.

Marie was in the third grade and Julie was in the first grade. My children were teased and picked on a lot and I didn't know how to protect them. One day, out of the blue, I had this idea. There was one little boy that used to come around our apartment who talked an awful lot. He was about 8 or 9 years old and seemed to know everybody's business, and he didn't hesitate to say what he knew about anybody's business. So one day I said to him, as if in confidence, "Do you know why we had to move here?" He was all ears.

"We moved here," I said, "because I killed a boy up in New York City. I killed him because he kept picking on my children. I killed that boy, but the police didn't put me in jail because they said I had psychological problems. To this day I cannot stand it when somebody messes with my children. I hope I don't have to kill another little boy or girl, but I will if I find out that somebody is messing with my children."

That's all I had to say. Nobody picked on my children from then on. In fact, after school, other children would run to me to tell me who was bothering my children and to let me know that it wasn't them.

I was still in therapy and on various medications for depression. As the months passed, things that used to be easy to do now seemed difficult. I only lived two blocks from the school. Yet, many times I would get my children to school late. Maybe up to 5 or 10 minutes late. I didn't mind when the school secretary said something to me, but I didn't like it when she would say things to my children about being late. It wasn't their fault.

I didn't know what to think about Tony. I felt like he was withholding money from us so that I would fail. I assumed he was angry with me for bringing our children to North Carolina. Social Services ordered him to pay $300.00 a month for both girls. We were never sure if or when it would come. If one of the children were involved in a special event and needed money for something, I would have to call him and remind him to send the $300.

Even though I wanted a divorce, I never had the money to pay a lawyer. Although Tony said he did not want a divorce, he was the one who found a lawyer and had the paperwork done. I thought that was odd, but didn't dwell on it. I was happy to read that we had 'joint custody' of our daughters. So I agreed to the terms. I had imagined that because of my mental health issues Tony could easily take full custody of the girls. What I would eventually learn is joint custody assumes both parents are taking care of the children.

In other words, I could not demand or sue for child support. Therefore, there was no way of getting money from Tony to help me support the girls unless he volunteered to give it. Lawyers told me that if I fought for full custody, then he would be forced to pay child support. I knew that would never work. All anyone would have to say is "Let's take a look at her mental health history" and I might never see my children again.

On the first of the month, we'd get our food stamps, and that was also the day Tony's check was supposed to come. On the first of each month I would dress myself and Marie and Julie up in our finer clothes. Sometimes I would make dresses for Marie and Julie especially for these occasions. I even called those activities the "first of the month events." Although I had financial struggles, on the 'first of the month' I would take Marie and Julie to see a show, or to a nice restaurant, or somewhere or to something that was really great. I didn't want them to be deprived of art and beautiful because of my mistakes. I didn't want them to have a 'poor' mentality.

Sometime for the "first of the month" events, I would go to the grocery store and buy each of us a lobster to cook at home. When I would take out my food stamps to pay for them, some people in line behind me would whisper that I was wasting their tax dollars. At that time I didn't know much about diet and nutrition, but even so, I fed my children mostly vegetables and fruits. I never thought that eating a lot of meat was a good thing. None of us were big meat eaters, in fact, none of us ate very much at all. We weren't into junk food and soft drinks. I didn't party at clubs or buy alcohol or cigarettes. So, let us have this lobster in peace.

The three of us were different. Each of us had our own style which was not the style of anybody else, anywhere else. We had great fun together. Sometimes in the evenings we'd have Club Night. Club Night was when each of us would take turns performing as if we were in a club. We would take turns introducing each other. Our life was not all sad.

At the end of each school year, Tony drove down and took our daughters back to New Jersey with him for the summer.

In the summer of 1990, Nelson Mandela, who'd recently been released from a South African prison, was touring the United States. Buses were leaving from Greensboro to take people to Atlanta to see him and hear him speak. I thought this would be a good opportunity for me to sell some hats and accessories.

I would arrive early and set up a display where people would be coming to wait for the buses. Surely I should sell a few hats this way? Although street vending was very common in New York City, I'd hardly seen any at all in Greensboro. This was good, I thought. I would show up and there would be no competition.

Shortly after I arrived at the parking lot that morning, a balding, yet handsome black man pulled up in a beat-up gold colored van and started setting up tables too. He looked at me and I looked at him and we each pretended we were much too busy to be bothered with the other.

He was selling T-shirts with empowering slogans on them such as, "Do for self or die a slave." He had lots of other shirts with pictures of Nelson Mandela on them as well, and books he'd written about ancient Egypt. I did sell a lot of hats and jewelry.

However, he "cleaned up" with the T-shirts. After the buses left, we started talking. He was an assistant professor at A&T State University and a writer and teacher of Kemetic or Ancient Egyptian history. His name was Dr. Ridgely Mu'min.

As I thumbed through some of his writings, I found what he had to say really interesting. I didn't know if I agreed with him or not. I wasn't even sure what he was talking about. But it was a whole new world—ideas—and concepts I'd never heard about and I wanted to know more.

Before our conversation was over that day, we decided to try joining our street vending forces. If I sold one of his T-shirts or he sold one of my hats, we agreed to pay one another a sales commission. In the beginning, we worked together. He taught me what he knew about the street vending business and African and Egyptian cultures. I taught him what I knew about merchandising and fashion. I expanded my line to include afro-centric and tie-dyed garments.

I started attending some of his lectures. He had a large following of black students who were hungry to learn from him. He had written a book called "AMEN: The Secret Waters of The Great Pyramid." In the book, he shared his theory that the pyramids were part of a water irrigation and purification system. I loved hearing all these new ideas from him and his students. It was a reminder to me of how awesome the world is and how little I knew about it.

While all of this was going on, I was seeing a therapist at a local clinic for the depression and mood swings. Most of the time I felt good and even excited about selling and the new people I was meeting. I was taking about three different medications—one for depression, one to help me sleep and one for anxiety.

This same summer I got a job as a supervisor with the 1990 census bureau. I was assigned a staff of about 15 people. Their job was to tally results from the census forms. My job was to make sure everyone fulfilled their quota each day. My shift started at 3 o'clock in the afternoon and ended at 11 p.m.

I enjoyed the people that worked with me. I told the people I supervised that we could have a good time as long as at the end of the night we'd met our quotas. There were some who were slower than others. We all helped each other. We laughed, brought in snacks, I never timed anyone's break and we always had our quotas and more.

Someone reported to *my* supervisor that I wasn't strict enough and my shift was talking too much, and that I had people on my staff who were not capable of doing the work and that I should fire them instead of 'babying' them. My supervisor could not deny that my team over-produced. However, she told me I would have to fire the woman who didn't hear or read very well. I told her I would not fire her. So, she fired me. She thought I was too soft to be a

supervisor, but the office was in need of a reception-
ist. She offered me that job.

It was fabulous. I dressed really nice each day
and wore one of my hats. I sat in the lobby of a build-
ing in the middle of downtown Greensboro. I had a
great view of Elm street. People passing by, including
policemen, would come in and talk to me. We'd talk
about everything from politics and movies to fashion
and how to stay motivated. People would bring me
food and offer to put money in my parking meter for
me. However, I never forgot that I was working, and
would politely ask people who seemed like trouble-
makers to leave.

Nevertheless, someone reported to my supervi-
sor that I was having too much fun and not taking
my receptionist duties seriously enough. My duties
were to greet and welcome visitors. I was told I was
no longer the receptionist. However, I was not fired.
They gave me a desk inside the offices, but never gave
me anything to do. Day after day, I'd show up and sit.
I guess it was like being in detention.

I kept getting paid my supervisor's salary and I
kept going to work to do nothing. I thought this would
be easy. However, I found it difficult to go to work
everyday to do nothing. I wanted to do something. My
bosses knew this. It seemed that keeping me doing
nothing after I'd been a supervisor and the reception-
ist was supposed to be some kind of embarrassing

punishment for not being strict and mean like they were.

Before I left New York, Luther told a friend of his about my hats. She saw them and loved them and even bought one. His friend introduced me to her friend who was Susan L. Taylor of *Essence Magazine.* During the time when I was going to work to do nothing, I learned that one of my hats had been chosen to be featured the coming fall in the November 1990 issue of Essence. I decided not to go back to the census bureau job. I would work exceedingly hard to promote my hats and accessories. I also continued to work with Dr. Ridgely.

The Joint Is Jumpin'

At the end of each summer, Tony brought Marie and Julie back to Greensboro a few days before school was to start. I was always tremendously happy to see them. They were anxious to tell me about their summer in New Jersey and New York. I was anxious to tell them about some of my Greensboro summer adventures.

Sometimes, time seemed to stand still. And other times, like when I'd look at how my daughters had grown, time was passing much too quickly. Marie and Julie were both good students who loved to learn. I put my kids through a lot with all of my mental health episodes. I lost count of the hospitalizations and the different medications I had experienced since our move back to North Carolina. Many times it was as if my children were my parents.

Marie and Julie always loved to dance. So, they would choreograph amazing dance routines and I would make these fabulous costumes for them. My all-time favorite was when they danced to Fats Waller's *The Joint Is Jumpin'*. I made a red satin dress for Julie and a green satin dress for Marie. Both dresses had sequins and rhinestones. And, each had a matching small pillbox type hat with a short matching veil. They performed at their school events and various events in the community. My children participated in a lot of fantastic activities.

They were versed in all styles of music, and Marie was quite accomplished on the viola that my mother bought her. They were wonderful children and are wonderful people today. Had my children not been so wonderful, if they were terrible people, or children that were always in trouble, I would understand that too. They have a good excuse not to be good people. But somehow they beat the odds.

This school year I was pushing myself extra-hard to get my children to school on time, street vending more days, and trying to find out how to promote my hats and accessories. I was taking my medication, including the one that was supposed to help me sleep, but I wasn't sleeping at all.

One day while the children were in school, I went to my regular therapy appointment at the mental health clinic. My therapist—not me—went in to see my doctor, and came out with a prescription for medication for me. I looked at the paper and could tell it didn't say Prozac or anything else I had ever taken. I thought the doctor had made a mistake. I said to the therapist, "I need to see my doctor, this isn't right. I need a new prescription."

"The doctor is busy," she said.

I stood in the middle of the clinic hallway near his door and called my doctors name out several times. I knew he was in there alone. Yet, he didn't respond.

"Dr Gray, I need a new prescription. This is not the medication I take." There was no response from the doctor, and my very own therapist called security to come get me. As a mental health consumer, you learn that once security is called, it's pretty much over—you are going to be locked up somewhere; either jail or a hospital. I was handcuffed and my feet were shackled. I was placed in a van and taken to a state hospital in Butner, North Carolina.

Butner was about 66 miles from where I lived in Greensboro. The ride to Butner always seemed painfully long. For one thing, I was always hand-cuffed and shackled. I always felt like a real criminal during my trips to this hospital. My mother was notified that I was admitted. I did not see a doctor until the next day.

Around noon, a staff member led me to a tiny room. With the exception of two chairs, it was bare. She said, "The doctor will see you now," and left me standing just inside the door. The doctor was writing something on a pad. He didn't say anything. I assumed the empty chair was for me and I sat down. He was wearing tennis shorts. I said, "I don't know why I'm here. All I wanted was for my doctor to give me a new prescription. The one he gave me didn't say Prozac."

He didn't even look up at me. He was still writing when he said, "Medicaid is not covering Prozac at this time."

I was in the hospital for two more days before I was released.

Crowns War and Art

As soon as the November issue of Essence hit the stands, I went out to buy it and look for my hat. I found the page where the hats were. The title on the page was *We Wear the Crown.* Instead of being called hats, the hats featured were called crowns because they were all styles that stood up high on a woman's head. (A la early Queen Latifa).

The reversible crown I had designed was a soft, quilted fabric of shades of grey abstract afrocentric designs on one side. The reverse: the finest quality solid black velvet. The hat could stand up like a crown or be pulled either forward, back or to the side like a beret.

Immediately orders started to pour in through my contact information listed in the back of the magazine. I hadn't anticipated this. I didn't have the money to buy in large bulk to get the materials at a good price. I sold many hats. However, it was a great opportunity lost because I wasn't ready, so there was not much money made on that venture. I thought it was interesting that almost all the orders I received for my hats were from women in the military, who were either involved, or about to be involved in the Persian Gulf War in some way.

I was exhausted. After the great hat rush, I didn't want to do anything. But, I had to keep going. I would often cry for no visible reason. My mother began to nag me about getting rid of my locks and straitening my hair. She would come to my apartment anytime she pleased and just let herself in without even knocking. She totally ignored any and all rules I had for my children, and did whatever she wanted to do. Tony was calling more and more and quizzing me on what was going on in my life. He told me that I was not to have a boyfriend or bring another man into his daughters' lives.

One day, while Marie and Julie were at school, I threw all of our glasses, one by one, on the kitchen floor. I didn't clean the glass up. I just kept looking at it. I thought it was beautiful. When Marie and Julie came home and saw the broken glass and that I wasn't interested in cleaning it up, they looked confused, but not surprised. It seemed, they accepted the idea that their mom did unexplainable odd things sometimes. I told them it was art. "I was just expressing myself." We ate at Wendy's for two days. The day my mother found out about the glass on the floor, I became a patient at the state hospital in Butner again.

My mother didn't like driving long distances or driving at night. Yet, no matter how far away a hospital was that I was in, she seemed always to find her way there. She also took care of my children whenever I was *away*. Sometimes she would come to visit me and I just didn't want to see her or anybody else. But she kept coming back.

After two weeks I was released. I was on some new and different combinations of drugs. I felt weaker and more tired than ever. I had given my mother, my children, and Tony good reason not to trust me emotionally. I was a failure. I really did want to do good. However, for the most part, my thoughts and actions went against the norm. What was I supposed to do? How come all of the therapy sessions and all of the medication wasn't making me well and normal?

For a few weeks, I didn't feel like leaving my apartment. The children's school was having a carnival type event. They wanted me to take them. Marie said, "Just take a whole bunch of medication, mama. Then you'll feel better." She made me smile. I pulled myself together and we went. We had a great time. I loved that my children still loved me.

One time I was trying to avoid having a total meltdown. I thought I'd 'head it off at the pass' so to speak. So before I did something that would get me in trouble, I took myself to a private hospital in Greensboro. I was immediately admitted. I was taken to a room and a staff member was sent to help me unpack my small bag. Just as I was getting settled, another staff member rushed into the room and said, "She doesn't have the insurance she needs to be here." They helped me repack my bags and sent me on my merry way with no referral, no medication, no nothing.

Some of the hours, days, and the weeks of my hospital stays all blur together. There were times when I knew I had been in the hospital, but I had no recollection of anything that happened there. I remember being discharged from at least two hospitals with no recollection of the discharge. In other words, I was home, but I couldn't remember how I got there.

Not that I had a choice, but there were some hospitals that I preferred over others. I liked the hospitals where they would just leave you alone. Sometimes I appreciated the hospitals where the staff was too small and overworked. At those hospitals nobody bothered me about going to group and music or art therapy. I would just take my medication and do whatever I wanted to do, which was usually nothing. That suited me just fine.

During one of my hospital stays, I decided that I shouldn't be there and they were holding me against my will. I went to a pay phone on my floor to call a Mental Health Advocate I knew of. I dialed information for the number. But the operator said the number too fast. I dialed again. But she said it too fast. So I called again and said, "Please, you're saying it too fast! I don't understand!" But she said it too fast again. I took the receiver, and I hit the phone. I hit the phone! I hit the phone! I hit the phone! I was immediately surrounded by hospital staff. They pulled me down the hall and pushed me into a small room. They left me in the room by myself because, one of them said, "You are too angry to be with other people."

One time in group therapy, I don't remember what we were talking about, however, I said, "This country could bring back slavery, anytime it feels like it." My therapist told the doctors what I'd said. They decided I was delusional and gave me more and stronger medication. My doctor told me that if I thought I was going to get too excited, to ask the nurse to give me my pill.

So, a few days later, something happened that made me angry. I'd learned that being angry in a mental hospital is not a good thing. Any emotional outburst—even if justified was usually taken care of with more medication or physical restraints. I told the nurse what my doctor had said and asked for one of my pills. She wouldn't give it to me. So I went to my room and I slammed the door. She said, "Don't you slam that door."

I slammed it again.

She said, "You better not slam that door any-more!"

I slammed it again and again and again and again and again and again and again. Four people came and got me and carried me to a room that was away from the others. They tied me to the bed!

Sometimes, if the hospital staff thought I might be having suicidal thoughts, I was put on suicide watch. If you were on suicidal watch you were not allowed to have your regular clothes—just hospital gowns and robes. When I was off suicide watch my mother would bring me my regular clothes.

I do have one pleasant memory that stands out above the rest. The time a nurse said that if we took our medication and didn't cause any trouble, we could go on this bus ride. For some reason, I was excited about that. One evening, a group us (women) were led outside to a parked bus. We filed on the bus. The bus driver's name was George. Some of the ladies were saying, "George, if you just want to drive me right on back to my house in Greensboro, that'll be all right with me. I'll give you a little something for gas."

George drove us all around Durham so we could see the Christmas lights on people's houses. I never felt such peace as I did that night just riding on that bus looking at all those pretty lights. I never wanted that bus ride to end. Neither did any of the other ladies. They were saying, "Take your time now, George, take your time," and "Take the long way back, George. Take the long way!" But, George brought us right on back to the hospital.

It was the same old routine day in and day out without any answers or any cure, just pills, more pills. The test for going home was whether or not you could remember what day it was and who the president of the United States was. Sometimes they would take us on an outing and observe how we behaved. Usually the outing was bowling. To this day, I hate bowling because of this. The truth is I never liked bowling, however, I knew they were watching me so I had to pretend I was having a good time so they would write something good in my report that would allow me to go home. I hated bowling then, and I hate it even more now.

One of my scariest hospital stays was during a period when I was vegetarian. My Goodness! The staff and the patients both were mad at me. The patients kept trying to fight with me because they said I must think I'm too good to eat meat. Then, either the staff didn't know what vegetarian meant, or just totally didn't care. For that hospital stay, every single meal I was served a bowl of grated cheddar cheese and nothing else—every single meal—grated cheese—nothing else.

I have to mention the time a cafeteria worker told the women on my floor he was a doctor. He was always in our rooms and asking us personal questions about our lives and families. There are things that go on in the hospital that many of us just don't mention or we try to forget.

To report a crime, like rape, for instance, would mean that you first have to admit publicly that you were in a psychiatric hospital. I've talked to women who talk about being raped in mental hospitals as casually as they talk about taking their medication. To report it, of course, becomes your word against the word of someone respected in his or her profession, and who holds a full time job. Some battles aren't worth fighting, or are they?

It's Called Bipolar Disorder

One summer while the children were with Tony, instead of using the time to rest, I was trying to do a million things at once before they came back. I wanted everything to be perfect when they got back. I felt a need to prove to my mother, my children, their father, my brothers and sister—and myself, that I was really okay—that I was getting better—that I was worthy. I worked myself into frenzy. By now, I was on eight different medications. Some were for the mental illness and some were for the side-effects of the medication for the mental illness.

I took the medication that was supposed to help me sleep but sleep would not come. Sleep was a stranger to me. In an attempt to just get some sleep, I took more and more of the sleep medication, one pill at a time. I waited to see if I was getting sleepy. I was not. I kept taking the pills through out the day until I had taken the whole bottle. Nothing happened. I still wasn't sleepy. I was awake all night.

The next day I had a meeting with a woman who asked me about making custom shirts for her family reunion. I also met with some students at A&T State University about making costumes for their upcoming step show. That night my body started to go limp and I was dizzy. I had gone 24 hours before feeling the effects of the bottle of sleeping pills—and feeling like I was going to die.

I don't remember the trip to my local hospital emergency room. When I regained consciousness, the doctors said there was nothing they could do for me. The medicine had been in my system too long. They left me in a room by myself. I was sure I would die.

My only concerns were Marie and Julie. *They would be better off without me. If I were out of the picture their father would take them out of the projects. Maybe they would live in a big pretty house somewhere.* I waited to die.

As daylight became visible, I sat up. I started cleaning my hospital room and even made my bed. I went into the day room and straightened up in there. As other patients started coming into the day room, I convinced them to let me fix their hair. I styled hair most of the morning.

I then started counseling the other patients about how to deal with their problems, and even made a few calls down to the billing department to let them know to at least wait a few weeks after we got home before they start bugging us about our hospital bills. That was one of the main complaints patients told me they had. I felt, if given the opportunity, I could run the whole hospital single handedly. I was feeling good. In fact, I felt great!

Later that afternoon, my doctor and another doctor I'd never met before called me into a conference room. One of them said, "Aren't you the lady who came in here last night as a result of an overdose? Only a few hours ago, you tried to kill yourself."

I said, "It was a mistake. I just wanted to go to sleep. Everything is all right now. I feel good now. I'm ready to go home now."

My doctor said, "I don't know how you are still alive."

I said, "Thank you."

"Don't thank me. Thank God. God is why you are alive."

However, after I was discharged, this very doctor sent me a bill for a humungous amount of money. Did he think *he* was God?

A few other doctors came in and all of them started questioning me about different things. They asked questions that none of the other doctors and therapists had asked before. I told them about the California trip. I'd never told a doctor or therapist about the trip I took to Los Angeles when I was at NYU before. I'd only told all of my previous doctors and therapists about feeling depressed and sad and feeling like I didn't fit in anywhere and about the every day stresses I was dealing with.

The next morning they invited me to a meeting with four or five other people.

Someone said they thought I'd been misdiagnosed all these years. "It's not just severe depression that you are dealing with. You have bipolar disorder."

Someone else asked, "Do you know what that is?"

"Is it the same thing as manic depression?" I asked.

"Yes."

"I read about that in a book by Patty Duke."

"Well we're going to start you on something called lithium. We believe this will help stabilize your moods"

"Will I be cured?"

"There is no cure for bipolar disorder. You will have to be on this medication for the rest of your life. How do you feel about that?"

"Well, I'll do whatever it takes to feel better. Imagine all these years—it took all these years for me to finally find out what is wrong with me."

I was diagnosed with bipolar disorder in 1992 at the age of 42. The doctors seemed happy. I was happy. Finally, there was a name for it. Manic depression. Bipolar disorder. I had a name for it!

After the doctors left, a woman stayed behind to talk to me about returning to school and learning something that would allow me to find work easier. She said that when I'm discharged, they would like for me to enroll in the North Carolina Vocational Rehabilitation Program. She said this program could help me get back in college if I wanted to, and it wouldn't cost me hardly anything at all.

That sounded like a great idea. I'd never gotten my degree from NYU because I started working in shows. I always enjoyed learning. Wow! What would I study in college this time? Fashion. Textile and fashion design. Within a few months, I was a textile and fashion design major at the University of North Carolina at Greensboro (UNCG). Shortly after that, with the help of a lawyer, my disability claim was approved.

I was told I could work as long as I didn't make more than a few hundred dollars a month. I worked a little with Dr. Ridgely with the street vending and also attended his lectures when I found the time. He didn't care one way or another about my mental health issues. He was supportive; however, he didn't seem to believe much in mental illness. He would always say to me, "You do not want to kill yourself. You really do want to be around to see how all of this (meaning world politics, science, religion) is going to turn out. Just stick around. I think you'll find it all very interesting."

Today, I find myself saying that same thing to other people. "Stick around. I think you're going to find it all very interesting." I'm so glad to have known Dr. Ridgely. He made me curious about myself, life and the world we live in and how amazing it all is. He also taught me *that truth is often stranger than fiction.*

As-Salaam Alaikum

One Saturday night, Dr. Ridgely called me and asked if I could go to the Nation of Islam mosque on the following day. He made it all sound so urgent. He told me what time to be there that afternoon. I said okay. He hung up and that was the end of that conversation. I knew where the mosque was, but I'd never been inside.

In my search for that thing that would save me, I'd studied a little bit about Islam, Buddhism, Baha'i, Hinduism and re-visited Christianity. Things that had to do with Dr. Ridgely, I'd come to just see as adventures. My visit to the mosque would be another adventure. I was curious as to why he wanted me to come, and why it sounded so urgent. I assumed he was going to be speaking and wanted to make sure he had a big audience.

I pulled into the parking lot in front of the mosque right on time and saw some beautiful black men in dark suits and bow ties. Two of them rushed over to my car and opened the car door for me before I could. They greeted me with, "Good afternoon ma'am." When I stepped inside the mosque there were two young ladies dressed all in white—including white veils on their heads. They said for security reasons they would have to pat me down.

One of them took my purse and peeked inside and the other patted me down as if looking for weapons. I stepped inside. It was smaller than I had expected but decorated very nicely. The men were sitting on one side and all the women were sitting on the other side. I sat down and kept waiting for Dr. Ridgely to appear. I found the service quite enlightening and empowering. I enjoyed the speakers. I didn't see or hear any evidence of anybody hating anybody. I found the whole experience pleasant and I found the people to be warm and friendly.

I decided I would go back again. When I finally spoke to Dr. Ridgely, it appears he never had any intention of coming to the mosque that day. He wanted me to experience the mosque for myself without his influence. It worked. Every time the doors of the mosque opened after that day, I was there.

I met a woman named Janice at the mosque. Janice and I hit it off right away. She became my best friend. We are still great friends to this day. She had two children and was pregnant with her third. She attended the mosque with her husband.

Janice was curious like I was. We wanted to know everything that was going on, not only at the mosque, but in the world. We wanted to contribute and make a difference too. I found out many of the ladies at the Mosque were interested in sewing. So for a while on Saturdays I taught sewing classes. Marie and Julie used to come with me to the mosque. The women are taught a dress code of modesty. For the Sunday meetings I would dress them in all white and the traditional veil covering their hair. They liked the idea of wearing the veil. Most of the time our white garments were made from sheets I had redesigned.

My mother was nervous for us. There was so much negative media about Minister Louis Farrakhan and the Nation of Islam. The media said the Nation of Islam was dangerous and full of hate. I found it to be just the opposite. I found it peaceful there. I met men and women who were just looking for ways to improve their lives. My experience with the Nation of Islam was actually quite enjoyable. As with any organization there were, at times, personality conflicts, and there were a few people on 'power trips'. I thought they were too strict on women about what they could or could not do.

People would ask, "How can you expose your children to the Nation of Islam? They preach hate. They say, 'the white man is the devil'. Aren't your children half white?" I would say, "First of all, since I've been going to the Nation of Islam events, I've never heard anyone preach hate. And secondly, people also say 'Man went to the moon'. Does that mean *every* man went to the moon? When I hear the phrase, 'the white man is the devil', I take it to mean that the white man has done a lot of devilish things. I don't think anyone can deny that—especially if you are black and living in America."

"However, it does *not* mean that *every* white man is the devil anymore than 'man went to the moon' means that *every* man went to the moon. I realize that if there were not some compassionate and supportive white people—if there were not white people who also died during our battles to be free, we would still be slaves."

Marie, Julie and I attended many events where Minister Farrakhan spoke. These events were peaceful and joyful times for us. We would meet women and children from all over the country. We'd share information about childrearing, schools, different businesses, health tips, recipes, and how to be independent people. When we'd hear about the event on the news the next day, it would be reported that it was an event that focused on hate.

They would show clips of Minister Farrakhan and other speakers out of context. They would show a few out-of-context clips that didn't sound too pleasant and say that the whole event was about those few words. Marie and Julie would say, "That's not what happened." Even my children noticed how the media could spin a story and have you believing whatever they want you to believe. I consider that one of the most valuable lessons my children ever learned.

I had been a member of the Nation of Islam for almost a year when, I came to the conclusion that the

Nation of Islam was not something I could give my whole life and soul to. Like any other church or religious organizations I'd experienced, I needed to be more in control. I could not follow rules blindly. I wanted to make the rules. I am grateful for the experience and the lessons my daughters and I learned there.

Black until Further Notice

When I received the first disability check, I received an extra large sum because it had been determined that I had been disabled a few years prior to when my claim was approved. I was determined to save for a rainy day, so, for the first time since *The Wiz* tour, I had a savings account. However, I wanted to do some special things for my children and my mother.

I took my mother to a sewing machine store and told her to pick any sewing machine she wanted. She chose a very simple, no frills machine, and seemed quite happy. I enrolled Marie and Julie in a summer music camp which was held at UNCG each summer. They stayed on campus in the dorms with other children their age from all over the country.

I also took them shopping and let them pick out whole outfits from their favorite mall stores. We'd never done that before. Usually we bought a skirt or a pair of pants or a sweater, but not a whole outfit at one time. As we walked through the mall, I asked them to tell me if anything 'spoke to them'. When they would see an outfit in a window they liked, I would go in the store and say, "I want that outfit the mannequin has on."

The store clerk would say, "Do you mean the skirt?"

I'd say, "No."

"The top?"

"No. I mean the whole outfit, including the stockings and the shoes and all of the accessories."

I bought myself a computer.

Finally, I'd be able to financially take care of my children.

As Marie's fifth grade year was ending, there was a certain middle school I wanted Marie to attend the next school season. This school was considered a magnet school. I didn't then, and still don't understand why some schools should be considered better than others and receive more money. Why not make *all* of the schools equally as good?

Anyway, even though I didn't get it, of course I wanted my daughter to attend this school that got a lot of money and had state-of-the-art learning equipment. I went to a meeting about how to register my daughter for the school, and at the end of the meeting I was told the school had reached its quota for black students for the coming year, and by law, and in order to keep the school politically correct and diverse, they were only registering white students at this time.

Since my ex-husband, Marie's father, is white, I thought to myself "No problem." I had always considered my children black because historically in this

country if you were not 100% white, you were black
or at least 'other'. But in reality, I thought she could
be whatever race she wanted to be since she did have
a black mother and a white father. She could choose.
In fact, I don't see why any of us can't just choose
whatever race we want to be. My children used to
jokingly refer to themselves as "Blite."

So, while some woman was still rambling and
apologizing because all of the students who applied
would not be able to attend this very fine school, I
leaned across the table and whispered to Marie, "How
would you like being a white child for a while?" She
said, "Cool." Julie, who was sitting beside me, asked
me, "Am I white now too?"

I said. "No. You're still black until further no-
tice." I enrolled Marie in the school as a white child. It
was settled. When the children would return for the
next school season, after spending the summer with
their father, Marie would be attending Lincoln Middle
School.

I was enjoying my classes at UNCG. However,
the algebra was kicking my behind. Time was really
flying. My second college semester was ending. Marie
and Julie's fourth school season in North Carolina
was also ending. When we arrived, Marie was in the
second grade and 'miracle baby' Julie was in Kinder-
garten. Now, Marie was getting ready for sixth grade
and Julie would be in the fourth grade next year.

It was a gorgeous spring morning the day I went to take my finals for the semester. When my finals were over and I went to get my car, it was gone. Students always parked on this side street, but today all the cars were gone. I asked a policeman about the cars. He said they'd all been towed. Then he pointed to a sign that said towing zone.

I'd never had a car towed before, and wasn't sure exactly what I was supposed to do. The policeman said I needed to go down to the police station in order to get my car back. So how was I supposed to get to the police station if I didn't have a car? I asked the police officer if he would give me a ride. And he did.

When I got to the station, I filled out the necessary paperwork and I believe the fine was around $80. I wasn't happy about that, but I was ready to get my car and go home. So after I paid my fine, I asked where I could get my car. Then another officer tells me that I have to go down to the car pound and pay them another $100.00 to get my car.

Well, that's when I lost it. I wasn't just thinking about me. I was thinking about all of the other students whose cars had been towed. I was thinking about anybody whose car had ever been towed. It was all so unfair. How do you get ahead if with every step you take forward, someone is dragging you back two steps? I'm a good citizen. I'm doing the right thing. I was in school. My head was suddenly filled with all of these thoughts about how unfair life is. I thought paying the fine would be enough. But now I see that I have to pay even more money to get my car back. Who thinks up these things?

I suppose everything would have been all right except I was not just thinking these things. I was saying these things out loud. One officer said if I didn't be quiet they were going to arrest me for disturbing the peace. He said, "Lady, say one more thing and I will arrest you." Well you know I had to say it. I had to. I said, "One more thing."

The next thing I know, I was in handcuffs. The officers kept asking me my name. I thought this was ridiculous in as much as I had just filled out all these papers with my name and address and anything else you could possibly want to know about me. Yet, they kept asking me my name. I said, "My name is Lonnie Anderson and when Burt hears about this, he is not going to like this one bit." (I was referring to Lonnie Anderson and Burt Reynolds who were a high profile celebrity couple at the time.)

I was taken to the room where they process you before they put you in jail. They took my backpack and while searching through it found bottles of medication. So instead of arresting me, they called my house. Marie answered the phone. Then he spoke with my mother. I was taken to a nearby hospital where I spent a night.

My hospital admissions had become routine. It was what I did. No one was surprised anymore. From time to time I was admitted to various psychiatric hospitals. That was my life.

I started concentrating on getting my daughters ready for their visit to New Jersey. When the school year ended, I packed up some of their things and their father drove down from New Jersey to pick them up. They were excited and I was excited for them.

The summer passed quickly. I missed them terribly. I bought them new school clothes and I found a new kind of barrette for their hair. The barrettes were flowers and butterflies made of silk. I had all kinds of presents and goodies for them. I had spoken to them periodically during the summer, but not every day.

The day before they were to come back I called to see what time I should expect them to arrive. I first spoke to Marie. She didn't have much to say. That's not like Marie. I asked to speak to Julie. Julie did not say one word.

"What is going on? Let me speak to your father."

Tony got on the phone.

"Is everything okay? What's going on?" There was silence. Now I yelled, "What is going on there? What's wrong with Marie and Julie?"

"I have decided that I'm not bringing the girls back."

"What do you mean you're not bringing them back?"

"I'm keeping the girls up here."

"No!" I screamed, "You have to bring them back!"

"I'm not bringing them back."

"I'll come and get them!"

"No. The girls will be better off up here."

I don't remember what else was said or not said. I called my mother. She told me Tony would be coming to town to get Marie and Julie's things. It seemed to me like they all knew. They all knew.

The day that Tony came to Greensboro to get Marie and Julie's things, I was held in a room in the mental health clinic where I went for therapy. They were afraid I might try to harm him. In retrospect, perhaps holding me there was a very good idea.

Later that day a sheriff took me back to my apartment. There are no words to describe the pain, anger, frustration, and fear that consumed me. I felt betrayed by Tony and my mother, and yes,—even my daughters. I felt completely alone. When I walked into my apartment, I saw the pictures of Marie and Julie that were on the living room wall. As I looked at their faces, I cried uncontrollably.

I missed them and I wished they would come back. After a while, I could no longer look at their pictures. It hurt too much to think I might not see them again. As tears streamed down my face, I took the pictures down and threw the framed photos in the trash can. I then got all of my photo albums out. I tore-up every picture I had of my children. There was even a haunting thought that they no longer loved me. I spent the night thinking of ways to kill myself.

The next morning I could not shut down the thoughts in my mind. *What do I have to live for now? I am a stupid, gullible, worthless being. I cannot do anything right. I am a poor excuse for a human being. I caused pain and embarrassment for my family. I am a failure at marriage. I failed as a mother. I was embarrassed for my old theater friends to see how I lived. I*

needed to kill myself as soon as possible. I'm crazy.
My doctors told me I'd be crazy for the rest of my life.
Nobody cares anything about my pain. To the world,
I'm just a lazy bum on welfare. I am a crazy woman
who is unlovable. I deserve to die.

Later that day, my mother came by. She was concerned that I wasn't eating and brought me cans of something called Ensure. She made me promise to at least drink the Ensure even if I didn't have anything else. I was angry with her and I couldn't hide it. I didn't want to see her that day and I told her so. She suggested I call my therapist for an emergency appointment. I don't remember all the details, but within a few days (yeah, you guessed right) I was admitted to a psychiatric hospital. This one was in Greensboro. After about a week I was released with some new additional drugs.

I did nothing except stay in my apartment. My mother brought me food. The combination of medications made me feel tired and sleepy, so it was easy to train myself to sleep almost around the clock. When I was awake, I watched TV. Television was my companion. I never turned it off.

I surfed—channel to channel to channel. I didn't have the patience to sit through a whole show. I felt even more ashamed and foolish when I would see some of my old theater friends in movies and TV shows. They somehow had held on to their dream. They were happy, successful and beautiful. I hated myself even more. I skipped the news all together. I didn't want to know what was happening in the real world. I did stop at the home shopping channels where I knew all the hosts by name.

The shopping channels were there for me 24/7. Lots of smiling faces and pretty things. They couldn't see me, or judge me. Back then, shopping by TV was still a new phenomenon. There weren't the amount of people shopping by TV that there is today, so when I called in to talk to one of the hosts on the air or to make a live testimonial, I usually got through. When I bought some great earrings and talked to the nice host about what outfit I was going to wear them with, I wasn't mentally ill, or a mother who couldn't take care of her children, or depressed, or over-medicated—I was just a friendly woman with good taste.

My counselor from the NC Vocational Rehabilitation called and suggested I return to UNCG for the fall semester. I told her I was too depressed. She said that was exactly why I should go back. I worked closely with the disability office at the university. They were kind and had me check in with them on a regular basis. If ever I didn't show up when I said I would, they came looking for me. Anytime anyone mentioned my children, my eyes would swell with tears. Although I was still angry with their father, I tried to hide it because I didn't want to be given more medication for that too. It was hard to stay angry with

Marie and Julie. I started keeping in touch by sending them comical and colorful newsletters I made on my computer about what I was doing and what was going on around Greensboro.

I was an emotional wreck. I cried easily and I barely ate at all. My classes did give me other things to focus on besides my personal problems. My therapists and counselor at the school were concerned about me getting through the Christmas holidays without my children. During the winter break, they arranged for me to check in by calling a certain number at the psychology department office every day by a certain time. I was told that if I did not call they would send the police to my house. The Christmas holidays were sad and lonely. By the time the break was over, I was emotionally and physically drained. I told everyone I needed to take the next semester off.

It was there in my public housing apartment that I was planning my 'final curtain'. I was ready to check out. I didn't know how to do life. I was ready to get it over with. I felt that if life was a game, I was never going to score another point.

One evening, in the background, I heard some man talking on TV about how you can improve the quality of your life if you bought his audiotapes. It turned out to be this infomercial and everybody in it was talking about how happy they were that they listened to this man's tapes. I was annoyed with him and his tapes and all the smiling people around him. What a contrast between his lifestyle and mine. There he was flying his plane and hanging out on Fiji Island. He was getting on my last nerve.

I took a closer look and noticed his good looks and how very tall he was, towering over his audience. He smiled a lot so it was hard to miss his big teeth. But I figured he would look silly if he had normal sized teeth because everything about him was big. Why is everybody so happy? He's a con artist. How can you change your life with some audiotapes? I changed the channel, but I kept changing back to see what the man was saying and if the people around him were still happy. I shouted out loud to the TV, "Yeah. Right. This is silly. I would never order you audiotapes in a million years." I paced and watched, and paced and watched some more.

I was intrigued because these people were living how I wanted to live. I wanted what I saw and I didn't know how to get it. Their lives were all happy and good and they were all smiling and having fun. They weren't worrying. That was it! That is what I found so disturbing—no one was worried. But if his tapes worked so well, then why didn't anybody tell me about them—my doctors or social workers? Why didn't they tell me I could feel better with these tapes? This is ridiculous. I thought. But then I listened some more.

He talked about "the power within each of us." I sat on my couch and got madder and madder at him telling *me* that I could be happy if I just did what he said? "Who are you to tell me I can be happy?" I screamed at the television. "I am unhappy and I can't get happy by listening to your tapes!"

Finally, I told myself, I would order the tapes to prove this man wrong. Yeah. That's it. I would show him to be a fake, a phony and a fraud. I would save other innocent people and their money from this con man. To prove him wrong I had to do everything he said, to the letter, so when I sent my report in (to whomever you send reports of this nature) I could say that I did everything exactly as he prescribed.

I found my debit card and I got on the phone and I bought Mr. Anthony Robbins' tapes. I paid the first of four easy payments. Before the last payment, I would have already proved him wrong and returned the tapes anyway. So, no money lost.

When the tapes arrived, I ripped open the box and started on my mission to prove Mr. Robbins wrong. I carefully read the instructions and did everything step-by-step, and then I started listening to the tapes. And the greatest thing about tapes, was that I could just listen. I could just lie down on the couch and listen. It would be easy to do everything he said and prove him wrong.

Immediately, I liked his voice and energy. The doubt was still in my head that this could help me, but I couldn't help liking him. I liked how he put things. I wanted to keep listening. About the second day, I turned off my TV. After I saw where he was going and things started to click for me, I remembered I had heard the same kinds of things from Reverend Ike at the Mind Science Church in New York when I use to attend with my children.

Rev. Ike taught, "You can be what you want to be, do what you want to do, and have what you want to have." I had forgotten about these sermons and how fantastic they made me feel. I felt comfort when Rev. Ike quoted the Bible, "And do not be conformed to this world, but be transformed by the renewing of your mind . . ."

I loved the things he said; however, at that time, I was concerned about paying rent and having food to eat. One of my biggest challenges was getting my children to school on time. I didn't have time to figure out how to "renew" my mind.

I have heard and now believe, "When the student is ready, the teacher will appear." Now, the Tony Robbins' tapes were reminding me of that power again—the power within me. This time I was ready.

Nevertheless, I felt I'd made too many mistakes. Because of my mental health situation and the stigma that came with it, I felt my life was pretty worthless. I felt hopeful again when among other things, the man on the tapes explained, "The past does not equal the future." Just because my past was lousy didn't mean my future was going to be lousy too. I started believing it.

I was a "Why me?" person. I was constantly asking myself, "Why am I suffering like this?" "Why can't I always have lots money?" "Why do I have to take all of this medication?" "Why am I so stupid?" "Why? Why? Why?" I heard the man on the tapes say, "If you want better answers, ask better questions." I learned that the universe / God will give me the answers to whatever I ask, so why not ask questions that would give me empowering answers? So I replaced the "Why me?" questions with *How* can I feel stronger?" "*What* can I do to be happy?" "*How* can I stay out of the hospital?"

I also learned that by changing how we physically carry ourselves, we can change how we think and feel. I started behaving the way I wanted to feel. I was *acting as if.* In other words, I walked and talked as if I were well—as if I were successful—as if I were healthy and happy—as if I were beautiful. I was working from the outside in. When I forced myself to smile, I couldn't feel depressed. The psyche doesn't know the difference between what is real or imagined.

I listened to the tapes for more than 30 days. Instead of the TV, I was now playing the tapes 24/7. I woke up to the voice of Tony Robbins. I fell asleep to the voice of Tony Robbins. I couldn't get enough of hearing how wonderful and powerful I was. This was about the time I thought I'd be writing my report of how this man was ripping people off with his audio tapes and then 'check out' of this life.

Instead, I put my suicide plans on hold. I was excited about living again. One of the most powerful and thought-transforming statements I heard on the tapes was, "Your illness may be *what* you have, but it is not *who* you are." And then Mr. Robbins asked the question, "Who are you?" I didn't have a clue.

I started looking for other authors and material that could shed some light on this subject. "Who was I?" I didn't know exactly who I was. However, right then and there I decided I was *not* my illness. I knew I could not, and would not let mental illness control my life or define me any longer.

I read more books and listened to other tapes that shared more information about the human potential and how other people had overcome challenges that were far worse than mine. I became fascinated with the power of my own mind and understood I'd never *really* tapped into it. I started reading about people who were getting relief from various health issues by using only plants and herbs as our ancestors did. I developed an interest in alternative health treatments and the mind, body, soul connection, and I was learning about the power of words and goals and visualization. The tapes introduced me to many new ideas, and I was just *crazy* enough to believe I could change my life.

I am frightened at how close I came to ending my life. I truly believed I had nothing to live for. I believed I would never know how to be happy. I had made too many bad decisions. I not only decided to live, but to live well. Dying and death would always be there. I could choose to die at any time. I'd been close to death many times. I never went through with any of my suicidal plans because I think I was more afraid of death than life.

From some of the other materials I was reading I learned that my soul could not die. Only our bodies can be destroyed, not our spirits. Death no longer frightened me. When I was no longer afraid of death, I was no longer afraid of life. I would live. But this time it would be on *my* terms.

I changed my perspective about myself. For instance, I was *not* stupid. I did some stupid things. But the stupid things I did in no way define who I was. I have always been a magnificent child of this loving universe—a queen. That time they tied me to the bed in the hospital—I was just a queen tied to a bed. I didn't know that then, but I was learning these lessons now.

I also knew I would have to go out in the world and put my new thoughts into action. There is a big leap from thinking you can do it—to doing it. And what was 'it' anyway? I had to figure out exactly what I wanted. There was a question that resonated in my head day and night. Almost every book or tape I listened to either asked it straight out or alluded to it. The question: "What would you do if you knew you could not fail?"

Well, I would be an actress again. I wanted to get back on the stage, but I had been away from New York for almost ten years. All of my old agents and friends had either moved on or passed on. Although I could pass for younger, I was in my late forties. In the theater, that is considered old. I also thought if word got out that I had been in mental hospitals, no one would hire me—even for the ol' lady roles. I would have to regroup.

The thought of going to therapy frustrated me because it side-tracked me from my forward progress. But while in the 'system', I was required to continue therapy and stay on my medication. In group therapy, we rehashed the same problems and whined about what was wrong in our lives, and what was wrong with the medication, and what was wrong with our doctors—and you see where this is going? By then, I was on another wavelength.

I wanted to talk about what we are capable of despite our illnesses. I wanted to discuss plans that went beyond finding the right medication and getting stable, which were our goals. How bizarre it suddenly seemed, that our goals (collectively) were to become and remain stable (it's no wonder some patients commit suicide). I was so sick of being sick and afraid, and focusing on our fears in group therapy. Although the leader tried to get us onto self-esteem issues, we always stayed buried in our problems and fears. Some people were truly terrified of their parents dying, and wondered who would take care of them.

People in the group thought I was doing great. At least I knew where my children were. I could at least pick up the phone and call them if I wanted to. Most of the mothers had lost legal custody of their children to family members or foster care because of too many extended hospital stays or irrational behavior.

I was in a new place (physically and mentally) and I wanted to talk about hope and progress; I also realized these people were my friends so I didn't want to downplay their feelings. However, I used my desire to perform to try to improve the atmosphere. I did stand-up and told jokes about our conditions and our financial woes and I got everybody laughing—except the leaders. They were convinced that I was acting out the manic in my manic depression. But I didn't care what they thought. People in the group were having a good time and I was back on stage and I was no longer ashamed of myself or afraid of the challenges ahead.

I continued reading and studying about personal power. The books and tapes I listened to also talked about forgiveness. I was reminded that my being angry with someone did not affect anyone but me. In order to feel good, I would have to release all those negative feeling—not for their sake, but for my own health and happiness.

I was reminded that I not only had the power to forgive others, I had the power to forgive myself as well. I would stop letting the actions of others determine how I felt. Eventually, I was able to say out loud, "I forgive me" and mean it. It was difficult, but I knew I had to stop being angry with Tony and my mother. I wanted to feel good. I wrote letters that no one would ever see where I asked for forgiveness and I forgave everyone who I had issues with.

I listened to or read books by Wayne Dyer, Deepak Chopra, Dr. Frederick Bailes, Louise L. Hay, Queen Afua, Orisison Sweet Marden, Ilyana Vazant and others. I was interested in anything that was about human potential. I immersed myself in more and more books, tapes, anything that kept reminding me of how magnificent I was—anything that motivated me to love and honor myself.

While dealing with my illness in North Carolina, I never ventured far from my apartment except to go to a doctor, or to therapy, or to a hospital or a state office or court. Now that I was feeling stronger I was out and about more. Although people were friendly, I started hearing people whispering my story.

"Girl, I heard she was in a mental hospital."

"She used to be on Broadway; now she lives in public housing."

"Well, I heard she was on welfare."

I was not going to let anyone else tell my story. That was *my* story. I would tell my own story of how mental illness interrupted my life. In fact, that's what I'd write about. I'd write and perform a show about how mental illness interrupted my life. Not just a show—I'd write a musical. Then, in the future, if I ever heard anybody say anything about my mental illness, I could say, "I already told y'all that. Didn't you see my show?"

I started talking about my life with mental illness—out loud. When I was at UNCG, a few of my classmates told me it was not wise to let people know I had any mental health issues. You'll never get a job, they warned. However, I realized that half the stress of the illness had been in trying to hide it. At the mental health clinic where I was receiving treatment, I was brave enough to ask for an African-American female therapist. I had never had one before. I'd had a few white female therapists. I had white male therapists most of the time. They were okay, but I didn't feel like talking to them about female issues, ex-husbands, and being black.

I knew that asking for a new therapist could backfire, but I pushed for it. Over the course of my treatment, I had encountered many health care workers who were "sistas with attitudes." Fortunately, I liked my new therapist, Nancy. She kept her professional distance but she treated me like a friend. We talked about our families and guys and carried on general girl talk. That was what I needed then. I needed a friend. For the past few years, I led a secluded life. In the meantime, I started writing my one-woman musical.

From my new collection of books and tapes, I was hearing about how meditation was helping a lot of people. So, well, you know, I had to try that. I knew a little about meditation from when I explored Buddhism and other religions. And I'd read that chanting and meditation helped Tina Turner turn her life around. So I figured there must be something to this meditation thing.

In a used book store, I found a set of tapes called the *Silva Mind Control Method* by José Silva.

Using the tapes I taught myself to meditate. I was learning how to be in control of my own mind. José Silva grew up poor but he had a special gift. He was not able to get a formal education but he had a secret for learning. He believed people could learn more effectively in a state of meditation or, as he described it, at the Alpha level. From the *Silva Mind Control Method*, which is now called *The Silva Method*, I learned about brain wave frequencies. Brain waves have been grouped according to their frequencies and labeled with Greek letters. The most common frequencies include Alpha, Beta, Delta, and Theta. For instance, when our brain waves are at the Beta level we are highly alert and focused; Alpha, we are relaxed but alert. In Theta, we're drowsy (also first stage of sleep). When we are in Delta, we are asleep.

José Silva noticed that when he read lessons to his children while they were in the Alpha state, they retained the lessons better. In some instances, while at Alpha, they were able to tell him what he was going to ask before he even asked it. *The Silva Mind Control Method* taught me that through meditation one is able to tap into the genius within. I'm only expressing a mere inkling of the wealth of practical information and wisdom that the *Silva Mind Method* offers.

To this day, when I want to create something, I lie on my sofa with my eyes closed and start imagining what I would like to see. Without thinking about it consciously, I go to the Alpha state that José Silva talked about. When I was creating the show, I laid on my sofa and imagined the show that I would like to have seen or see about mental illness and bipolar disorder. As scenes or monologues would unfold I would go to my computer and write them out. Most of the songs came to me while I was in the shower. I remember jumping out of the shower dripping wet looking for a pen to write:

> *Everything looks so familiar to me*
> *I've been at this place before*
> *I really thought I was going somewhere*
> *But I'm right back at the very same door . . .*

I'd also sing the melodies into a recorder so that later I could remember how the tune went. I could hear the songs in my head complete with orchestrations; however, I didn't know how to notate what I was hearing on music staffs. I was driving on Interstate 40 one night when just out of the blue, I started singing:

> *Why can't you fix me—fix me—fix me*
> *Ain't that what doctors are supposed to do*
>
> *I've never missed a single appointment with you*
> *I've been to every therapist that you've sent me to*
> *I've taken every pill that you told me to take*

I try to get my rest I don't stay out too late

Why can't you fix me—fix me—fix me
You're my doctor
Ain't that what doctors are supposed to do . . .

Every hour I was awake, I worked on my show. Going to therapy and taking medication was now a nuisance. I finished my show in about three weeks. I didn't know writing a play was supposed to take a long time. In addition, I really didn't have anything else to do. In the very first version of the show, I had original songs, but I also threw in a couple of old-school R&B songs that I'd always wanted to sing. It was a blast! I had so much fun. I was not in this world. I was lost in a beautiful creative world.

Before long I had a show that I thought was good. Among the many working titles were *Sick But Not Shut In* and *A New Way of Flying,* but *Balancing Act* was the best, so it stuck.

I wanted to make my play better so I joined a playwriting workshop called The Greensboro Playwrights Forum. The people there were interesting, friendly and helpful. I enjoyed being a part of their group. They helped me understand more about the art of playwriting. For the first time, someone other than me read my script.

Different members gave me ideas about how they thought I could make it better. They would invite me to hangout with them after the meetings at a nearby cafe. I felt proud. I was hanging out with people in cafes! I was a part of a group—and it was not a mental health therapy group. (I had come a long way, baby).

I approached a couple of hospital special event offices and then talked to someone at the local Mental Health Association about the show I had written. No one was interested in the least. When I told Nancy, my new therapist, I had written a musical about my mental illness and I thought it might help some people, she took me seriously. She even gave me the name of an organization that she thought might be interested in my work.

I looked at the name and the number on the card. I'd never heard of the organization before. National Alliance for the Mentally Ill - Guilford County. I called the number the next morning. The pleasant woman who answered the phone gave me the number of another friendly woman named Elaine Purpel. Elaine told me The National Alliance for the Mentally Ill (called NAMI for short) was a grass roots organization that gave support to mental health care consumers and their families. I told her about my show.

"Your show sounds wonderful. I would love to see the script."

Although the script was not in perfect form, I took it to her anyway. She called me about a week later and said, "The NAMI - Guilford County members are very interested in seeing your show." She said they would surely come if I invited them. Okay. Now what? How would I make this happen? I was actually hoping that this organization was going to help me showcase it.

When I told the playwright's forum members what she said, they volunteered to help me set up a showcase for *Balancing Act.* Stephen Hyers, the director of the forum, did all he could to make the showcase a success. He was incredibly generous and helpful. They would provide a theater space, lights, sound equipment and somebody to operate them. This was exciting.

Willing To Take That Chance

On the road to my goal to perform, I gained confidence in my questioning. I knew I didn't want to go to therapy anymore. I got far more out of my hour if I listened to Anthony Robbins or studied nutrition or worked on my script. So, I pushed the next envelope—straight at my doctor. I also knew I did not want to be on the ridiculous amount of medication that I was prescribed.

Prozac made me feel euphoric; Lithium made me feel jittery, made my hands shake and caused my thyroid to go out of balance, so I took a medication for my thyroid called Synthroid. Then I got off the Lithium and took Tegretal, which made me break out in hives, so then I went on Wellbutrin which is an antidepressant, then Clozapine—which is an antipsychotic. I ended up back on Lithium. I was told Lithium was best for me, and my thyroid situation would be okay as long as I kept taking the Synthroid as well.

Here is a list of some of the other drugs I was on from time to time: Elavil, Haldol, Klonopin, Mellaril, Naven, Norpramin, Tofranil, Trazadone, Valium, Depakote and Lorazepam. While in the hospital I was never sure what I was taking, so there were probably others along the way. This list does not include non-psychiatric drugs that I took to alleviate the side-effects of various medications. No subtraction—just drug multiplication.

I became curious about a health food store in the community where I lived and went in several times before I actually bought anything, or talked to anybody who worked there. In the beginning I would memorize the names of some of the things on the bottles and then go home and look them up on the internet. After a short while, I felt I knew enough to ask questions that sounded halfway intelligent. I met the owner whose name was Art. I liked him because he assured me right away that no question is a stupid question.

He explained some of the herbs and how people use them. He talked about the importance of keeping the inside of our bodies clean as well as the outsides. After a few visits I started telling him a little bit about my bipolar diagnosis. He, like Dr. Ridgeley, didn't make a big deal about it.

He said, "I know of a combination of herbs that might help you." I knew I was in a store whose purpose was to make money. I knew I didn't really know this man, Art, so I was a little leery at first. And then I thought, "Could this bottle of herbs be any worse than all of the other stuff I was taking? What if it *is* something that can help me?" I wasn't sure what it was, but he told me the name and explained the properties of each herb. I hesitated for a moment. "Should I take this stuff?" And then I thought to myself, "I'm not sure what all of the medication I take now is, and nobody ever explained what the ingredients were in them and where they came from."

"I'd like to have a bottle." I said. The bottle cost me $40.00. I'd read in a book entitled *The Serpent and the Rainbow* by Wade Davis that the first psychiatric drugs were based on a Native American herb. I remember wondering at that time, "Why not just use the natural herb?" Maybe I was finally on to something. When I got that first bottle of herbs from Art, I was still going to the clinic and taking medication, so it was hard to tell if the herbs were working or not. I wanted to see if the herbs alone would really make a difference.

I was educating myself about herbs and diet and natural treatments. More and more, nutrition is being used to treat physical and emotional illnesses, and I found a diet devised for cancer patients. If it can help them, why not me? Only after a few weeks of eliminating all sugar and white bread products, I felt more alive and energetic. I was living proof that change in diet was working, but when I talked to my doctor . . . well . . . it didn't go over very well, to say the least.

"Doctor, I want to try alternative treatments."

"You need to stay on your medication." He didn't even look at me.

"I've been exploring a diet that has helped cure cancer patients and . . ."

"You need to stay on your medication."

"Well I'm feeling much better after cutting out sugar and I've learned that if you can't pronounce an ingredient, then you shouldn't put it in your . . ."

"You need to stay on your medication to stay out of the hospital."

That was all that mattered to the doctor. Stabilize and stay out of the hospital. Once you've been diagnosed, it is your illness speaking and no one hears you—they just dismiss you—the person.

He started writing furiously in his notebook and looked at me as if I was really insane. "If you aren't going to stick to our plan and prescribed medications then we can not be responsible. We will have to close your case and you will surely get sicker and be worse off."

"Well Doctor, I am willing to take that chance." I said to him.

Big decision. Scary decision. But, I didn't think twice. It was an easy decision. And no one worked very hard to talk me out of it. I'm sure they were thinking, "She'll be back." Nowadays it isn't so easy to just stop your medication; sometimes they will come to your house and make sure you take it.

Oh, Jesus, what had I done? Were they right? The thoughts haunted me at first. Would I get sicker and eventually spend the rest of my days in a state mental hospital? I had gone off my meds before and I did get sicker. However, the times I had done it before were because I was fed up with the side-effects and fed up with doctors and I didn't care about anything. This time was different. I was taking positive steps to heal. I had goals. I wanted to get better.

Yes, I was scared, but only when I thought of what the doctors had told me—that I would probably get sicker. I was scared when I would hear a voice say. "There is no cure for bipolar disorder. You will need to take medication for the rest of your life." I was scared when my mother and sister asked, "Are you sure you know what you're doing?"

One of the benefits of being diagnosed with mental illness is, after a while, whatever seemingly bizarre thing you want to do, you can. If you do something others don't agree with they assume it's because you are just a very sick person and they leave you alone. By this time, my mother, my sister and the few friends I had were not surprised by anything I did. This turned out to be a good thing. It left me free to explore all possibilities without interference.

When I decided to change my diet for instance, when I decided I was not going to eat any sugar or white bread, when I decided I was going to be a vegetarian, they all just shook their heads and said under their breaths, "Poor thing. Will she ever come to her senses?" Because they thought I was a hopeless case, they backed off, and I had the freedom to reinvent myself. Their biggest concern had been my children, and now my family seemed happy that at least my children were safe.

I consciously set out on a mission. My mission was to reinvent myself. I would create a brand new me and a brand new life for myself. All of the tapes I was listening to and the books I was reading assured me that a new life was possible. The worst (and, yes, in my opinion, worse than death) thing that could happen would be my spending the rest of my days in some state hospital. I had nothing to lose and everything to gain.

The first days were not easy . . .

I didn't take my pills but I don't recommend that. (DO <u>NOT</u> STOP MEDICATION COLD TURKEY!) What I know now that I didn't know then is the havoc that a quick psychiatric medication withdrawal can play on, not only your body, but your mind, emotions and brain. The withdrawal symptoms can include dangerous psychotic episodes. If I had it to do again, I would wean myself off at a much slower pace.

Medication builds in your body, so the first or second or even third day off wasn't too bad, but then it happened. I knew there was going to be some type of withdrawal. I expected it, so I hung on. I was dizzy and nauseous and mostly scared because there was no safety net. I was on my own.

Then I lost my appetite. However, I was determined not to force myself to eat. Even before I met

Art, and before I started reading books on nutrition and health, I innately believed our bodies tell us when to eat and when not to eat. It was the same principle I used when my children were babies.

So, I was not following any rules now—except my own. I started listening to my body. I wasn't hungry for the next three or four days. Loss of appetite used to be a sign I was either depressed, about to be depressed, or in the middle of a manic episode. "I'll wait this out," I thought. I just had to stay in my house. I didn't want people to see me or find out how sick I was feeling. In general my body felt weak.

I lay on the sofa with my eyes closed and kept listening to motivational tapes. I did force myself to drink a lot of filtered water. I knew it was possible for the body to live many days without food. However, plenty of water was essential. If someone came around, I just tried my best to act as if everything was just great. During those few weeks of withdrawal, I gave the best acting performance I had ever given in my life.

For a while, even though I had the shakes as a side-effect of the Lithium, my hands started shaking even more uncontrollably. My old thinking said, "Call a doctor." But the new me said, "This is withdrawal. You're going to be all right. If you call a doctor, you'll be forced to take medication, plus they are going to think you're even crazier." Sometimes I thought I was going to die. I was not afraid of dying. I was more afraid of continuing to live my poor excuse for a life.

I was sick for about a week. It wasn't too bad. It was like having a bad flu, I guess. I was headachy, nauseous and dizzy. Maybe it was the flu. I don't know. But one day I woke up and the symptoms were gone. I was tired and had a dull headache for a day. A few days later I wanted to eat something.

I bought a juicer and started shopping at the health food stores for fruits and vegetables. My children and I had started eating organic foods, when we could. We could taste the difference. One of the hardest things for me was getting used to the taste of vegetable juice. Then I read about adding an apple as a sweetener. And that worked great.

As a believer in the mind-body connection, I continued to pay attention to what I ate and what I thought. I was interested in knowing what various so-called experts in the healing field had to say about being well. I used myself as a guinea pig to learn what foods and supplements and mental exercises would help me the most. I didn't keep any clinical records or anything like that. It was based on feeling.

If something made me feel good mentally or physically, I kept doing it. If I felt bad, I would decide what the culprit was and eliminate it. Even though I heard that keeping a journal was a good thing, most of my journaling turned out to be creative writing—mostly poems or the beginnings of short stories or songs. Sometimes I would just write pages and pages of the same sentence. An example would be: "I am

wonderful" or "I am healthy" or "I am loved and lov-
ing" over and over and nonstop for several pages.

As I continued studying the power of words, I
started to believe that each of our names carry a
powerful vibration. I read that in different cultures,
people change their names to reflect their occupa-
tions, or where they are spiritually. I'd never really
liked my name, John Ann Washington. It no longer
spoke to me or for me. I decided to get a new name to
go with my new life. I started searching books for
names and what they meant.

I decided I wanted a name of African origin. I've
never been to Africa and I couldn't speak any of the
languages. However, the first time I saw the name
Wambui, I felt a connection with it. I read that in
Swahili, Wambui means "singer of songs." I decided I
was Wambui. I then decided on a second name.
According to the books I was using, Bahati means,
"My fortune is good."

My daughters and I had started exchanging
phone calls on a regular basis. I told them about
what I was thinking of doing and asked for their
input. They liked the names that I'd chosen and their
meanings. They said if this is what I wanted, they
wanted it for me too. I went down to the courthouse
to make my new name legal.

Well, I'm sure you can imagine what the rest of
my family was saying about my name change—some
behind my back, and others (my mother) to my face.

It wasn't pretty. But I was stronger now. My biggest concern was the money. I was told I would need to hire a lawyer and I would have to come up with at least $700 in order to change my name. My mother felt the money would be a deterrent, and assured everyone this episode would be over soon.

However, when I inquired about changing my name, a clerk at the court showed me a book with the form in it. She showed me a machine where I could make a copy of the form. She told me how to fill it out and how to get it posted at the courthouse for the required 30 days. She said there would be a small fee to get a new birth certificate. I filled out the form and filed it myself. I never used a lawyer at all for the name change. After my request had been posted for the 30 days, I paid $30 and got my new birth certificate. My name was Wambui Bahati.

Like a dark heavy curtain that opens to reveal the opening scene of a sparkling Broadway show, I saw the bad being drawn away and the good shining through and coming to life. It was suddenly all there for the taking. What do I want? I wrote it down and I said it out loud.

"I want to be happy. I want to be independent—financially and emotionally. I want to be on stage."

It seems so easy to say now, but the most important decision I made was to do what I wanted to do, to try and become what I wanted to be. And to stop doing what I didn't want to do, to stop being what I didn't want to be. And most importantly—I had to stop trying to please everybody.

From all the positive books and tapes I was listening to, I was just starting to understand what might be referred to as the snowball theory. It goes like this: If you really focus on what you want to accomplish, you don't have to worry about *how* it's going to happen. If you take the first step, the universe or God will suddenly be there to help you with the next two; and events just snowball from there. To some this may sound like nonsense. However, I and many who are thriving will tell you that it works every time. Many times we get so caught up in *how* that we never move forward.

The snowball theory was definitely at work for me as I prepared to showcase my show. I knew what I wanted and how I wanted it to be and how I wanted the show to look. I was completely focused on the outcome, but I didn't have all the answers. However, I seemed to attract the right people and the right information or the perfect situations to carry me forward.

I realized I *did* have a safety net. I was learning to consciously step out on faith. I thought about all of the miracles that I'd experienced in my life in the past. But, until now, I never saw or really appreciated them as such. The times when I demonstrated with members of my community for equal rights, facing angry white people and dogs held at bay. Yet, I walked with the others with my head high. I was not afraid. Weren't we all stepping out on faith? When I persuaded my mother to borrow $100 to send with my NYU admissions application, were we not stepping out on faith? Was it not a miracle that I was still alive? There was something greater than me at work for me.

My mother was nervous. "What do you mean you're going to do a show about your mental illness?" She had my sister Roberta who lives in New York fly to North Carolina to be with her at the show because she was afraid of what the evening might bring. My mother would say, "Baby, now, I don't think you want to do this."

The day of the show finally arrived. March 19, 1997. I was 47 years old, but everything felt new to me. I felt like a prisoner who had been released after many years for a crime he didn't commit. That evening I felt undaunted by world events, unscathed by life challenges and the kind opinions of others. I, the other people, and the place felt surreal. Perhaps I was just dreaming all of this. Perhaps I was having a reaction to a psychotic drug that made me believe the things in my imagination were real.

I was in downtown Greensboro in the Greensboro Cultural Center on Davie Street. With the help of the forum members and other volunteers, we set up 200 chairs. I was thinking that was a lot. NAMI members from Guilford County would, at the most, be about 60 people. The show was open and free to the public. A store called Pier 1 Imports loaned me wicker furniture and props for my show. As the time neared seven o'clock, I went over some of the songs with the musician.

When there were only a few minutes left until the show, I peeped into the theater. All of the chairs were filled. There were people standing in the back. I wasn't nervous, I was excited. I was calm and at the same time energized and ready for whatever the evening would bring.

With the support of a keyboard player who tried his best to follow me, as I did not provide written sheet music and improvised, I took the audience on the journey of how manic depression had interrupted my life. Much of the show was exceptionally funny and, as you can imagine, because of the topic, much of it was not so funny. As I think back on that very early version of *Balancing Act,* it was more of a mental illness night club act.

When it was finished I felt good. I had done it. I'd had a good time. I didn't know what people would think. Too late to take it back. Too late to go back into the closet of the mentally ill and pretend I'm not one of them. I had publicly admitted I'd been in mental hospitals and mental institutions, that I had psychiatrists and that I went to group meetings for the mentally ill, and that I had taken countless numbers of medications for the depressed and psychotic to try to regain my sanity.

I bowed, and my head was forming my mouth to say thank you, when I heard the applause and everyone got out of their chairs and was standing. The applause grew louder. All I could say was, "Thank you. Thank you. Thank You."

Many people, after seeing my show, called me in secret, e-mailed me in code, or wrote me letters signed with initials and showing no return address. The letters said, "Thank you for telling my story," or "Thank you for telling my mother's story," or "my sister's story," or "my father's" or "my child's" or "my brother's story." Others said, "You are so brave to talk about it."

Shortly after that NAMI- Guilford County told me about an event they were planning for the coming January. It would be held at the Cultural Center also. It was an event called "Open Your Mind" and they wanted to feature *Balancing Act*.

So, on the afternoon of January 11, 1998, I presented *Balancing Act* once again. The following week, an article on the society page of the local paper said, "Bahati, a former Broadway performer, used her strong voice to touch, amuse and enlighten the audience that packed the Cultural Center . . ." My mother had attended that performance as well. My mother didn't like that I was being so public about my mental illness and other personal matters. I was aware that every time I tell *my* story, I'm also telling part of *her* story.

"Mama, what did you think of the show on Sunday?"

"I didn't like it."

"You didn't like it?"

I braced myself. My mother says exactly what she feels. Sometimes she says things in a way that can be hurtful. However, I wanted to know. I wasn't opposed to changing or cutting a specific part that made her uncomfortable. I also knew she could totally trash me and my show and leave me in tears.

"Tell me. What didn't you like?"

"It was too crowded in there. They should have had it in a bigger place." I paused and waited for the bomb. Then I started to smile.

"That's it. That's what you didn't like about the show on Sunday?"

"I could hardly move in there."

I relaxed and exhaled and continued to smile for the rest of the day.

At the afternoon rehearsal before I did the first public performance of *Balancing Act* for NAMI, I'd met a woman in the bathroom who was curious about my show. She came back to see it that night. After the show we realized we knew each other from doing Community Theater when we were in high school. (She had attended one of the all white schools.) We hadn't seen each other since we were in high school, and both of us had different names. She'd known me as John Ann Washington, and I had known her by her maiden name.

Cathie had shown great interest not only in *Balancing Act* but also in my well-being. Even though I had performed the show and my mental health secret was out, I still felt better being at home by myself than around people who had nice houses and cars and money—and their children. Plus, I'd spent so much time alone I had gotten used to just being by myself.

Cathie was always sending me a note or calling to remind me of an event she thought I might be interested in. She continuously sent me invitations and reminders to come to the book club meetings

that the Women Improving Race Relations sector of
the Greensboro Commission on the Status of Women
had. I ignored them. Then one Sunday afternoon, I
was feeling good and I was remembering the lesson
on many of my tapes that said it is important to
associate with the people who are doing, being and
having what I would like to be, do and have. I re-
minded myself that these ladies are not better than
me; we are all from the same source. They had made
different life choices than me. I was now making
better choices.

Each Sunday meeting was at a different mem-
ber's home. The first time I went, I left my home in
the projects and drove across town to a beautiful
home. I parked my Honda Civic, and went inside to
the book club meeting. Cathie introduced me around
and all of the women made me feel comfortable. I kept
in contact with Cathie and I went to other meetings. I
never, however, volunteered to have the meeting at
my home.

By the way, here's the story of how I came to
own my new 1997 Honda Civic:

The car I was driving had become unreliable
and unsafe. My credit was less than desirable. My
only income was my disability. I'd been to Ford and
Chevy dealerships. A salesman at each of them said
they could work something out with me. It either
involved a very high down payment or/and an ex-

tremely high interest rate. However, I really wanted a Honda.

In the mornings, after meditating, I started visualizing myself in the 1997 silver Honda Civic I wanted. Besides what I learned from the Silva Method tapes about visualization, I also studied two other books. One was *Creative Visualization* by Melita Denning and Osborn Phillips. The other was *Creative Visualization* by Shakti Gawain. Again, reading this material triggered something I'd heard Rev. Ike say years earlier. He would say, "I want you to go stand in the spot where you are going to park your new car."

A few weeks later, when I went to the Honda dealer, a pleasant looking white man, who looked to be about in his mid-sixties, with a big smile approached me with his hand already extended. "Good morning ma'am." He introduced himself. I shook his hand and said, "My name is Wambui Bahati." His eyes lit up and his smile grew even wider.

"I saw your show!"

"What?"

"I saw that show you did a few months back at the Cultural Arts Center. That was great!"

"You were there?"

"My daughter took me to see it. Wait 'til I tell her that I met you!" I sat down at his desk. At one point during our conversation, he did call his daughter, "You'll never guess who I'm about to sell a car to!"

Needless to say, I didn't have to explain my financial or work situation. He gave me a good trade in price on my old car. The down payment and the interest were reasonable.

I drove away in my new Honda that day.

I Forgot About My Power

The local chapter of the National Organization for Women (NOW) along with women from the Greensboro Women's Resource Center were making a trip to Washington, DC, to attend the *Women of Color and Allies Summit*. I was invited to join them.

"Travel and share a room with other people?"

I didn't know if I was ready for that. Performing is one thing. Being with people 24/7 and not being able to get to my home when I might want to was another thing.

"From North Carolina to Washington, DC, on a bus?"

What if I got crazy again? What if I got psychotic? I thought long and hard about my decision. Was I really normal now? People seemed to think I was. My life had changed so quickly. As I thought of riding in that bus, I thought of the times I'd been shackled and handcuffed and taken to the state mental hospital in a sheriff's van.

I had to remind myself that is not how I want to think. I reminded myself of all the lessons I was learning about the power of thoughts. What we focus on we create more of. Of course, I could make this trip to DC. I decided to have fun. And, I did. It was an incredible adventure. I even performed excerpts from *Balancing Act* at talent night.

When we came back from DC, the group of NOW members from Greensboro was a strong force. We decided our focus would be the new welfare reform that was being introduced. Many women on welfare were either not aware of the drastic changes that were going to be taking place or they were in denial. We wanted to reach these women and families and prepare them for the transition.

In the meantime, NAMI—North Carolina had heard about *Balancing Act* and saw a video of the show. Beth Melcher, who was executive director of NAMI-NC (sometimes refereed to as NC AMI) at the time, had a vision. She asked if I would be interested in doing a ten city tour of *Balancing Act* in North Carolina. Wow! That sounded exciting. She said I want you to get paid something. Imagine I was going to get paid for doing *Balancing Act*. I thought I was dreaming.

Beth said, "I want you to meet me in Raleigh and go with me to this foundation. I want them to meet you and I'm going to apply for a grant for your show for the tour."

This is part of what the grant application said:

In 1996 NC AMI joined with the national organization to launch the Campaign to End Discrimination, a nationwide effort to raise public awareness and understanding of mental illness and confront stigma and discrimination.

NC AMI requires a commitment of $15,000 to support a touring production of the play *Balancing Act*. This musical production, written and performed by actress Wambui Bahati, offers an opportunity to use the arts as a teaching tool, helping raise public awareness and understanding of mental illness. By chronicling her own experience with mental illness, Ms. Bahati confronts the misconceptions and stigma that surround mental illness. Support from the A.J. Fletcher Foundation would allow NC AMI to offer *Balancing Act* to ten North Carolina communities. Supporting funds would be raised in the communities where the production is offered.

* * *

I felt like I'd died and gone to heaven. Well, not really. In fact, I'd never felt so alive or so honored. NC AMI received the grant. I was introduced to a woman name Kerry Nesbit. Kerry, I was told, would be doing publicity for my show. (Imagine my own publicist. Was I hallucinating?) Kerry designed a logo, posters and a program for *Balancing Act*, wrote articles about me and set up interviews with the media in the 10 cities I would be traveling to, and helped me set up my first Wambui Bahati website. The grant was enough to pay me and one piano player.

NAMI-NC also produced a video entitled "Excerpts and Interviews." As the title implies, it is me doing excerpts from an early version of *Balancing Act* interwoven with documentary-style scenes showing me answering questions about my life and bipolar disorder. NAMI - NC and its local affiliates were interested in educating, breaking the stigma, and reaching out to the African-American community.

David Kaspar who won an academy award for his movie, *The Panama Deception* lived in North Carolina and was the person NAMI chose to film and direct the documentary. I had a ton of fun making it. NAMI members helped as well other new friends I'd made since doing the show. Beth said I was to retain all rights and have the freedom to sell them as I saw fit.

I continued to work on the script. I knew it could be even better. I'd gone through several different finale songs. I wanted the ending to be big and powerful. I lay on my sofa one afternoon and I remember asking my father. No, not *THE* father. My biological father who had died a few years before. I asked him what this song should be. I sat up and wrote:

> *I forgot to be joyful*
> *I forgot to rejoice*
> *I forgot—just don't be vexed by this material world*
> *Don't listen to ignorant men*
> *I forgot to remember that the answers are within*

I forgot about my power
I forgot about my strength
I forgot not to worry 'bout what you see
'Cause there's a whole lot more to me
I forgot to remember that the answers are within

I performed this song as the closing number in the show for almost two years before I fully understood how powerful it really is.

All was well except there was no sheet music. I didn't know how to write the notes down. The music was in my head and on a cassette recorder. When I'd done the show, most of the songs were either acappella, or the musician I had would improvise chord progressions to go with my melody lines as I sang them. But all of us involved in planning the tour agreed, the songs I had composed in my head and captured on a tape recorder needed to be transcribed so any piano player could play them, and they'd sound roughly the same in all 10 cities. To me, having a written score was just one more sign this was becoming a real, professional show.

For the first time in many years, I knew what excitement felt like. Then I hit the first challenge. I called around and got some estimates from local musicians and realized, I didn't have the money to pay for transcribing my compositions. But I was not worried. I was now armed with the wisdom that all is in divine order. So I kept moving forward and focusing on how fabulous the show would be if a pianist could actually play the songs.

New York State of Mind

My daughters came to spend a few weeks with me that summer. They liked the new car and they liked living in the Section 8 townhouse. I had graduated from public housing and was now in Section 8 housing, which, like public housing, is based on your ability to pay. The portion I couldn't pay would be subsidized by the government. However, with section 8, you are not confined to housing projects. You can often find very nice homes being rented by private citizens.

I moved into a two-bedroom, two-story townhouse. I had a patio, a fireplace, a washer and dryer *inside* the house and a small front yard where I planted pansies. They were also happy about *Balancing Act* and said they wanted to help any way they could. I was happy to be with them. It was a joyful visit that ended too soon. I told them, now that I had a good car, I would be driving to New Jersey to visit them often.

When Cathie heard that the local NAMI and I were trying to get the music transcribed, she decided to write a grant proposal on NAMI Guilford County's behalf to secure the funds to pay for the transcription. Unfortunately, most of the local musicians in

Greensboro who could transcribe the music also had other jobs, so the transcribing job would be stretched out over a long period of time.

But I knew of a musician I'd worked with a lot in New York. He was fabulous and a good friend. I knew he could transcribe my songs in a timely fashion. I called him and told him about the project. I sent him a tape. He gave a price of what each song would cost to be transcribed. The price was high but he was available and willing. I told him someone was applying for a grant that would pay his fees. He wanted $1,000 to start, and besides the tape recordings, I would have to come to New York to work with him.

Okay. New obstacle. Let's see. I needed $1,000 and a trip to New York City. I'd heard Anthony Robbins say something like this: "God is my supply. Great sums of money come to me instantly, under grace and in divine ways." I started saying that over and over. I went to my computer and printed it out on a page to hang on my wall. While my copy was printing Cathie called.

Cathie asked if I could get the musician on the phone. Cathie, the musician, and I did a three-way call. Cathie told him she was applying for a grant. He told her the same thing he had told me a few days earlier. He wanted $1,000 to start and besides the tape recordings, I would have to come to New York to work with him. She told him if the grant fell through, she would pay the tab. When he hung up, Cathie asked if I was sure he could do it. I said, "He's the best!"

That night Cathie had me on a train with her bound for New York City. My friend JoJo invited us to stay with him for a while. Later we stayed in a hotel in Times Square. While working with the musician each day, I got the idea to visit my old friend Eric Krebs and let him know what I was up to. I was a little nervous because I had left in such an unprofessional way. I wasn't even sure if he would still see me. He made me feel welcomed and comfortable.

I didn't go there with the conscious intention to do so, but I ended up with an appointment for a mini backers audition for *Balancing Act*. The musician and I played a few songs from the show. Eric optioned the show and mounted a showcase at one of the studio theaters at the John Houseman Theater Complex where I'd worked 10 years earlier and left because I thought *they* were trying to get me.

So, the stay in New York was extended. I had written music. The show was now in rehearsal for a New York City debut. Up until now, I'd always done *Balancing Act* with furniture and props. It was Eric who suggested that I just do the show with nothing more than a square wooden box he gave me. I said, "But . . ."

"Just do the show. Besides, if you're going to tour, you don't want to have to bother with all that stuff."

I was used to all my stuff. Now it was just me and a wooden box. Eric hired a director, a costume designer and had someone design lighting. Scenes were cut and other scenes were rearranged. Well, this is just their vision. I thought, "If I don't like it I can change it back."

The two performances at the Houseman were September 28th and 29th of 1998. They were a huge success. I remember after the curtain call after the first show, I went into my dressing area. I could hear the people clapping and calling my name. The stage manager came back to get me to take me back to the stage. I felt like I had done this before. I felt like I had dreamed this all before and now it was true. It was déjà vu. I felt wonderful.

Tony and his girlfriend brought Marie and Julie from New Jersey to see the show. Roberta and some of her friends attended. After the show, Marie and Julie were crying tears of joy and gave me big hugs and told me they were proud of me. Eric and I talked about the future possibilities for the show. However, nothing further ever developed there.

On the Road Again

It was at this time that I learned a major lesson about following you inner feelings or instinct. One day during rehearsals for the New York show, someone came into the theater and asked what the program should say about who wrote the music. Before I could say anything the musician said, "Music and lyrics by Wambui Bahati and (his name)." I knew that was wrong. My whole being said that's not right, but I told myself I would deal with it later.

Well, I almost lost *Balancing Act* because of that. Once the programs were printed, I found out the hard way, that legally that program could be used as evidence that I agreed with the musician that we *both* wrote *Balancing Act*. He even claimed the show was his concept. I had some legal battles to go through because of that. I also learned that whether someone is your friend or not, get a contract that spells out all details, even the ones that seem like obvious common sense. Write it all out. Be absolutely clear—friend or no friend.

The grant did come through from the Community Foundation of Greater Greensboro. Cathie and I remain great friends to this day. She never gave up on me, even when I used to ignore her calls and notes. She didn't acknowledge that I didn't respond.

We arrived back in North Carolina only a few days before the first show of the 10-city tour was scheduled. The first show was at Bennett College in Greensboro on a gorgeous Sunday afternoon in October. I was on the road again. Me and my box. A local keyboard player played the first show. My songs were on real sheet music!

Even though the sponsors expected me and a piano player to show up for the show, I liked the idea of adding drums and bass. When I'd written the show, I'd envisioned a whole R&B band. For the next nine shows, I hired and traveled with three musicians. That meant there was far less money for me, but the enjoyment I got from singing the songs with the three musicians instead of just piano was worth every penny.

Press Release:

Balancing Act

A One-Woman Musical Written & Performed by Wambui Bahati

In Balancing Act, Wambui Bahati shares her powerful personal story of growing up in Greensboro and launching a theatrical career on Broadway, only to have her success cut short by mental illness. Through monologue and song, she portrays her struggle with bipolar mood disorder—an illness she did not at first realize she had and, once diagnosed, did not want to admit she had. At times hilariously funny and always relentlessly honest, Balancing Act presents an intelligent, informative portrayal of bipolar mood disorder and its effects on Bahati's self-esteem, career, relationships and day-to-day coping. From her ordeal, she emerges with hope for her future as she comes to terms with her illness and with herself. Presented in North Carolina by NAMI North Carolina 1998-1999 Tour Dates: Greensboro NAMI Guilford County Little Theater, Bennett College Sunday, October 10, 1998, 3 p.m. • Durham NAMI Durham Hillside High School Saturday, January 16, 1999, 8 p.m. • Goldsboro NAMI Wayne County Wayne Community College Tuesday, March 23, 1999, 7:30 p.m. • Raleigh NAMI Wake County North Carolina Museum of History Sunday, April 25, 1999, 3 p.m. • Fayetteville NAMI Cumberland County Cape Fear Theater Thursday, May 13, 1999, 8 p.m. • Winston-Salem NAMI Forsyth Anderson Center Winston-Salem State University Friday, May 21, 1999, 8 p.m. • Asheville NAMI Western Carolina YMI Cultural Center Saturday, May 22, 1999, 8 p.m. • Burlington NAMI Alamance County Paramount Theater Monday, May 24, 1999, 7 p.m. • Wilson NAMI Wilson Playhouse Theater Tuesday, May 25, 1999, 8 p.m. • Concord NAMI Cabarrus County St. James Lutheran Church, November 14 1999, 3 p.m.

* * *

I noticed that in the beginning of the tour, everyone connected and concerned with it was very gentle with me. They didn't want me to get too stressed or do anything that might trigger an 'episode'. But almost immediately, most people forgot about that. I was the producer in every sense of the word. I called rehearsals and told the band when and where to arrive and what to wear. I made sure the local affiliate sponsors had food for my musicians.

What I would wear for *Balancing Act* has always been a challenge. The costume I ultimately ended up with was one that I had tailor-made for me. While I was working as an usher at the Coliseum in Greensboro, I saw Tina Turner's so-called farewell tour. There was a part in her show where she wore this black jumpsuit with an empire waist. I took a picture of it to a seamstress in Greensboro who made a maroon colored jumpsuit for me.

On a show day, I did not eat all day. Eating seemed to drain my energy. By just drinking a lot of water and sometimes fruit or vegetable juice on show days, I felt more energetic and my mind was clearer for the show. Also, if I wake up feeling great on the day of a show, I don't want to take a chance on eating something that might give me an upset stomach. After a performance, however, I am ready to eat anything I can get my hands on.

Although NAMI paid, it was my responsibility to pick up the sound equipment and return it before and after each show. Beth Melcher had sent each sponsoring affiliate in each city a detailed timeline / outline of how to present *Balancing Act*. This included, securing a space, distributing press releases, and introductions, all the way down to "flowers for Ms. Bahati." It was a great time for me. The NAMI families were wonderful to me.

I made a trip to Baltimore, Maryland. I left for Baltimore on a Thursday afternoon. This was the first time I was taking a trip by myself that didn't involve my children or a show. The event was not going to start until the next evening, but I was too excited to wait any longer. I didn't want to take a chance on something going wrong. I wasn't familiar with the streets of Baltimore so I gave myself plenty of time in case I got lost. I'd spent a lot of money to pay for the event ticket and the hotel. I'd dreamed of doing this for a long time. Now seemed like as good a time as any. This event didn't happen every day. But, by now I knew all to well to just keep stepping forward. I trusted God had my back.

It was dark by the time I arrived at the Hyatt Hotel. There was a prom going on at the hotel, so parking was difficult. I checked into my room, went out for food and then did absolutely nothing. I just sat in my bed thinking about how good I felt and how happy I was to be there until I fell asleep. Besides Marie and Julie, I'm not sure if anybody else even knew where I was.

The next morning I explored downtown Baltimore and had seafood for lunch. I made a trial run—

one block—to the convention center. I was told the doors for my event would open at 4:00 p.m. It seemed like time was passing so slowly. I wanted it to be 4 o'clock, but it was only two. At three, I just went back to the convention center and sat by the door and waited. I noticed I was not the only person sitting by the door.

Just before four, I heard a loud, energetic beat coming from the room. When the doors were opened, I walked in and just stood in the back for a while. I wanted to savor the moment. I scanned the room from one edge to the other—the lights, the sound equipment and outrageously large speakers placed around the room—A multimedia wonderland! I didn't want to linger too long. I wanted to sit as close as general seating would let me. The energy was high. There were hundreds of people swaying, tapping, clapping and dancing to the music.

At five, the volume of the music went down. A pretty, petite, blonde woman walked on stage. She talked a little bit about her husband and when she introduced him, the crowd went wild. I went wild too! Tony Robbins walked on stage. At first I clapped and yelled like everybody else. Then I stopped clapping. My eyes filled with tears. I was in the same room with the man I was going to report for being a fake, a phony and a fraud. Now, I was looking at all of his 'tallness'—live and in person. Imagine, all the time, I was the one who was the fake, the phony and the fraud because for so many years I had not been living the *truth* of who I was.

This was the man that belonged to the voice that for so many months I woke up to and fell asleep to. That was him. The man whose voice inspired me when I had forgotten how to inspire myself. I was so close to ending it all. "Thank you." He couldn't hear me. I know he is not *the* someone. I know there are so many who inspire and motivate and save the lives of others. I thanked him because he was *my* someone.

He spent most of the afternoon preparing us for the fire walk. At about 9:30 that evening, he told us to meet him in the convention center parking lot so that we could get used to the heat. Baltimore fire trucks were there. Yes. It was real fire—burning wood chips. The heat, alone, was almost unbearable.

We went back into the auditorium where he continued to prepare our minds, bodies and spirits to walk through the fire. It was about midnight when we all went back. Well, there were some who didn't want to do the fire walk. Each of us had to agree to the legal disclaimer. I wanted to do it. There were many rows of burning timber. Each row appeared to be about ten feet long. I found a line to get in.

My turn came up three times before I felt I was ready. Each of those times, instead of walking across the fire, I'd just get back in the end of the line. The last time my turn came around, I remembered everything he said about focusing, and I stepped out. I walked so calmly across the flaming wood. At the end, just as he had told us, someone grabbed me up, while someone else rinsed off my feet with a water hose to wash away any stray pieces of burning wood that might be stuck to my feet. I walked on fire! And that was just the first night! The four-day *Unleash the Power Within* seminar continued through Monday morning. That weekend was a breathtaking, uplifting experience. I'll never forget it.

My Livelihood?

With all the attention I attracted doing *Balancing Act* all over the state, it wasn't long before the local Social Security administrators who managed my disability case asked me to be evaluated by a doctor. Of course, there was no hiding the fact that I didn't take medication. A month later I was off the Social Security disability roll.

Meanwhile, other organizations had started calling me to ask if I would speak at their events. At first I would go for free. Then I got tired of going out and inspiring everybody and then having to make deals with the phone company to keep my own phone on. So then I started asking for money for my presentations. Still in the beginning it was not much. Maybe $50 or $100. I know that some organizations were upset that I would ask for money at all. Sometimes they would tell me how much it would benefit the people and I would go for nothing anyway. However, I didn't feel good afterwards. People were always telling me I had a gift—a way of putting things that made people listen and understand.

Well, now if I have a gift, there must be some value to it. I had no other income. This is how I was making my living. I'm sure if their boss were to tell them to come to work each day for no pay or perhaps $20 for gas, they would not be very happy. I eventually decided there was value in me and what I did.

This was my livelihood and I deserved to get paid. It got to the point where I would rather do temp jobs in an office than get on the stage, bare my soul, give the best show anyone could possibly give, and then go home with no money or have to chase down the money I did earn. Also, I think a lot of people would see me on stage for an hour or so, but not consider all the work that went into getting to that point.

Run and Tell Somebody

After seeing *Balancing Act*, some members of the Greensboro YWCA asked me if I could write something about Domestic Violence for the "A Week without Violence" event. I said yes. I had about a month to put it together, but somehow nearly the entire month had passed and, with only two days to go, I had nothing. I lay on my sofa, closed my eyes and imagined the show I would like to see. The greatest challenge for me was to get the audience to understand the viciousness of this crime and still make it entertaining. "I am domestic violence" kept coming to me. "I am domestic violence." I got up from the sofa and started walking around my house saying, "I am Domestic Violence. Y'all don't recognize me do you? The story of my life. Everybody always trying to pretend they don't know who I am. I am Domestic Violence."

I quickly got up and got a tape recorder. I recorded most of the script. The next morning I went down to the urban ministries. They provided food and clothes to those in need. However, on certain mornings, anyone could go there and get as many clothes as you could stuff in a bag for $1. My mother was a volunteer there. I would actually go there and get clothes for myself sometimes. I still own and wear some of the clothes I got in the $1 bags. My mother would pretend she didn't know me. I didn't blow her cover. There was a woman from her church there one day who recognized me and said something to my mother. My mother was embarrassed, but we both had a good laugh about it later.

Anyway, on this day I went to get costumes for my new presentation. I got jackets or shirts for all of the characters and found a grey cape for Domestic Violence. I had a pair of red lace gloves with the fingers out that I'd bought a while back from a next door neighbor who was selling things one day to support her crack habit. I went to Wal-Mart and got a coat/hat rack to hang the costumes on. I spent the rest of the evening rehearsing the show in my apartment.

I drew the characters from what I'd heard, seen and experienced. I'd never talked about the abuse from my first husband or the rape that happened at NYU. I allowed my characters to tell the stories. But it would be years before I would admit that many of the characters were really telling my own personal stories. People knew about my mental illness because of *Balancing Act*. However, nowhere in *Balancing Act* do I mention I had been a victim of domestic violence. I thought to myself, "How many personal dilemmas can I present to the public?" I'd still never dealt with the rape.

It wasn't until I read a book entitled *Project Girl* by the late Janet McDonald that I was able to come to terms with the rape ordeal. In her book, Ms. McDonald tells a similar story of a rape that happened to her while she was away at college. Many of the details were similar to what happened to me. As I recall, she tried to bring charges against the man who did it but could not get the charges to stick.

Although she was a "woman with a genius IQ", according to her book, after that incident, she suffered with depression and other serious mental health issues. As I was reading her story, it made sense to me that the rape played a big role in her mental collapse. I then started to think about the role that my being raped perhaps played in my mental collapse. I'd never even mentioned the rape in therapy. For some reason, once I read her story, my story was easier to admit and deal with.

Instead of being introduced, I told the program coordinator that I would like to interrupt the program as Domestic Violence. Only the program coordinator and the speaker before me knew about this plan. When the speaker finished his speech, he continued with a sentence about domestic violence which was my cue to start my performance. The speaker also agreed to make it appear that I was interrupting him. When I heard the speaker say the certain cue sentence, I walked onto the stage wearing the grey cape and red, fingerless lace gloves, "Well, well, well! Y'all don't recognize me do you? The story of my life. Everybody always trying to pretend they don't know who I am. I am Domestic Violence."

The audience was surprised and amazed. *Had this woman just interrupted the program?* There was complete silence and all eyes were on me as Domestic Violence. Everything was working just as I hoped it would. I walked through the audience, "You know what? If I were to run out into the busiest intersection in this town right now and scream, 'I am Domestic violence! I Am Domestic Violence!' there'd be those of you right there who'd pretend you didn't hear nothing—you didn't see nothing—you don't know nothing about me . . . I can literally get away with murder!" As I was finishing the Domestic Violence Monologue, I eventually made my way back to the stage where the coat rack had been preset with the jackets and shirts. I sang a song; a cappella.

> *Somebody run and tell somebody*
> *This ain't how it's supposed to be*
> *Somebody run and tell somebody*
> *I can't believe what I hear—what I see*
> *Somebody run on and tell somebody*
> *Too many people living in secrecy*
> *Somebody run—run on and tell somebody*
> *Too many people dying unnecessarily*

Each of the coats and jackets on the coat rack represented a certain character. I slipped each garment on and the character told their story. At the end Domestic Violence re-appeared wearing the grey cape and red gloves. Domestic Violence scooped up the jackets and shirts that I had let drop to the ground as I finished each story. Holding the garments Domestic Violence says to the audience, "It doesn't look like I'm going anywhere anytime soon 'cause you don't want to talk about me. You don't want to end the secrecy that surrounds me. You think I'm not a problem. I can go anywhere I want to go. I can do anything I want to do. You can't stop me. I am Domestic Violence!" I exited. The audience applauded. I'd assumed it was a one-time presentation. Little did I know that *I Am Domestic Violence* would become so successful. I have performed it at various events in cities all across the United States.

The local NOW (National Organization for Women) chapter who I had taken the bus trip with to Washington, DC, was moving forward with our commitment to enlighten the public about the new welfare reform agenda. Some of the new rules included requiring most recipients to work within two years of receiving assistance, limit most assistance to five years total, and let states establish "family caps" to deny additional benefits to mothers for children born while the mothers are already on public assistance. Again, the idea was to come up with a presentation that both gave the facts but was also entertaining.

I came up with an idea for a play (it was supposed to be a musical but most of the women didn't want to sing) called *Welfare Blues*. It was a collection of short scenes that not only destroyed myths about welfare and gave the facts about the new welfare reform, but also touched on human rights and how our country was really spending its money. One of my favorite scenes was when three of us were dressed in pseudo-evening attire, à la the Supremes, and performed a number called "How Can You Fight for Your Rights?"

We were introduced with a big musical fanfare as the Rights Sisters. ". . . and now ladies and gentlemen—just back from their European tour—here live and in person—it's Civil! Human! And Political! Ladies and gentlemen, The Rights Sisters!" We'd do some 'Diana Ross and the Supremes' type choreography while we sang a song that started with these lyrics, "How can you fight for your rights when you don't even know what they are?"

We performed the show at a few public housing communities and a couple of public libraries. After the performances, a panel of welfare, community, health care professionals and local politicians would speak and answer questions from the audience. We also provided snacks and limited childcare during the show so no one would have an excuse for not coming.

I had been performing *Balancing Act* less than a year, when I got a surprising letter.

The letter informed me that, "On behalf of the NAMI (National) Board of Directors, it is my honor to inform you that you have been selected to receive the 1999 Lionel Aldridge Award. This award recognizes an individual for his/her service, courage and leadership on behalf of people with mental illness." Lionel Aldridge was a defensive end on the Green Bay Packers team, who after winning three world championships, was later diagnosed as schizophrenic.

The letter said they would like for me to be their guest at the conference, but didn't mention how I would get to the conference. The conference was going to be in Chicago. Was I supposed to pay the expenses to get to the conference in Chicago where the award would be given? Was I also supposed to pay for the hotel?

I wasn't sure how to ask about the ticket. Did everyone else who had ever received the award have money to pay for their transportation and hotel when they got theirs? Was I just too broke? If I was broke, should I just have someone receive it on my behalf and not even bother to find a way to get there? The date was staring me in the face and I hadn't received any more information about the conference and didn't know what to do.

I called Kerry, the woman who had done publicity for NAMI for the North Carolina *Balancing Act* tour. We had developed a friendship. I asked her what I should do. I had some money coming that should show up in my checking account on the 2nd of July. However, I would need to leave for Chicago at least by June 30th, now only a week away. "You mean they didn't send you your plane ticket?" She said it like I should have known to ask for one. Kerry said that for sure this was an oversight. This was all new to me. She suggested I call them and tell them I had not received travel information or a plane ticket yet.

I called the number on the letter I'd received. I spoke with one of the organizers. "I'm excited about receiving the Lionel Aldridge Award."

I hesitated. "I was wondering . . . I mean, uh . . . I didn't know if your organization would be providing a plane ticket for me or not." I tried to make it seem like I was about to do it and I didn't want to end up with two tickets. She asked which North Carolina airport I was closest to and said I should receive an airline ticket in the next few days. I did receive the ticket as promised.

Now, I wondered about where I would stay once I got to Chicago. No one ever mentioned a hotel. I called Kerry again. "Kerry, should I just assume they have a room for me at this hotel?" I don't remember who called whom, but I received word from the organization that I had a hotel room.

I was no longer embarrassed about the mental illness thing; I was now embarrassed because I was so broke. I didn't party, eat out or eat very much, I didn't hang out in clubs or drink alcohol or do street drugs. My TV was off and I'd lost my interest in shopping from the TV, mostly. However, I couldn't go by a computer or electronic store without going in to check out the latest gadgets. I was still trying to pay off bills from the earlier, even leaner times. Mostly however, I was also investing and reinvesting money I had in ideas and projects that I thought might help me earn even more money in the future.

Financially, I was always playing catch up and I was tired of it. All the other areas of my life were developing beautifully. I could see the progress I'd made. Physically I felt great! I looked good too—even if I do say so. More and more people were inquiring about *Balancing Act* and other programs that I could do. I was driving up to New Jersey every 4 to 6 weeks to visit Marie and Julie. I was meditating and reading more about all kinds of natural solutions to various life challenges. Financially, however, I was still challenged.

Many of the NC NAMI affiliate members I had met during the 10-city tour called to congratulate me and wish me well in Chicago. I was too embarrassed

to tell anyone that I had less than $10.00 for this trip.
I decided I wouldn't think about how I would get from
Chicago's O'Hare Airport to the hotel in Downtown
Chicago. I just kept repeating "Everything is in divine
order. Everything is in divine order." It's a phrase I
say to calm myself when things appear to be going
wrong. I use that phrase to this day. If I'm ever run-
ning late, I repeat to myself, "Everything is in divine
time. Everything is in divine time."

When the plane landed at O'Hare and I re-
trieved my suitcase, I knew I didn't have enough for a
cab to downtown Chicago. I quickly figured out I
didn't have enough for the shuttle buses either. I
found someone who told me how to get to the hotel by
subway. Because I was used to traveling by subway
in New York, figuring out Chicago's system was easy
for me once I knew the name of the stop to look for.

After checking into the hotel, I decided to ven-
ture outside and explore downtown Chicago while it
was still light out. I'd been here several times with
Broadway show tours. This was a gorgeous, sunny
and hot day. I loved it. Every block seemed to have a
life-sized cow. There were cows everywhere. Each cow
was uniquely painted or decorated with bright colors,
designs and various themes. I learned the cows were
an art exhibit called Chicago's Cows on Parade. They
were beautiful and amazing. I walked from cow to
cow, all over downtown Chicago. By the time I got
back to the hotel, it was dark and I was hungry and

tired. I was alone and lonely there. I went back to my room, had a pear and went to bed.

The next morning I was up early. I went to search for where the plenary sessions would be held. Once I knew, I went back to my room and got dressed. I had a black crepe sheath dress with a matching jacket and black patent leather pumps I'd purchased recently for another *Balancing Act*-related event. After I was dressed, I looked at myself in the mirror and said, "Girl, I'm proud of ya'. You did good."

The lyrics to a song were coming to me and I started singing out loud. The song was coming out in response to a question that Tony was asking me lately. You see, Julie, who would be going into the 10th grade the following school year, told her father she wanted to come to North Carolina to live with me. It seemed all of his New Jersey family and friends felt this was a terrible idea and told Julie so. Tony asked me to talk her out of wanting to come and live with me, but I said, "If Julie wants to live with me, I welcome her with an open heart and open arms."

This answer irritated Tony. "What are your plans?" he kept asking. "What are your plans?" "What are your plans?" The counselors and therapist in New Jersey told Julie that I could get sick again. My answer was Tony could get sick or hit by a truck too. I asked him what his plans were. Of course no one took me seriously. However, I was not going to tell my child she could not live with me. So, as I stood in that hotel room that morning all dressed up, I kept hearing Tony ask, "What are your plans?" The answer that I wanted to give to Tony and Julie's therapist came to me in a song:

Julie,

I plan to pray for you everyday
And send plenty of love and light your way
I charge God Almighty himself to watch over you
night and day

That's what I plan for you
That's what I plan to do

I plan to share with you all the wisdom I know
Then step right back and watch you grow
I know the day will come when I'll have to let
your precious hand go

That's what I plan for you
That's what I plan to do

I checked my lipstick and went down to accept my award. I found the large ballroom where people were gathering. I sat down in the back. As the morning program was beginning, someone approached the microphone and asked the audience, "Is Wambui Bahati here?" I stood up. The woman walked off the platform and motioned for me to come down by the stage where she was. She was friendly and took me to a seat on the first row where she said I should sit.

Then the program officially started. The first award recipient accepted her plaque and then went over to the podium and gave a short speech. And the next recipient gave a speech, and the next. I bet you can guess . . . I didn't have a speech. Was I supposed to have a speech? Was I expected to say something? The other recipients had been either authors or professionals in the mental health field or both. Because I was not an author or a professional was I supposed to just smile, say thank you and then sit back down? Then the emcee called my name.

I guess it's one of those defining moments. I could have frozen or just said thank you and walked away with my award but I started talking. I was standing and walking the way I had practiced with those Anthony Robbins tapes. I thought to myself, "I am a magnificent child of the universe too." I looked out at the sea of faces. I think the presenter was surprised. She stepped back.

I thanked NAMI-NC for having the vision and trusting me. I talked about writing *Balancing Act* and why I wrote it. "Half the stress of the illness," I said, "Is in trying to hide the illness . . . When I hear people whispering, 'she used to be a star on Broadway, now she lives in public housing on welfare,'" "I want to be able to say, 'Didn't you see my show? If you had seen my show, you would have heard me when I sung I'm lonely po' an' sad.'" Then I burst into a song from the show.

> *I'm lonely po' an' sad*
> *My credit's really bad*
> *Somebody pinch me please*
> *I'm waiting in line for cheese*
> *How did I get so poor?*
> *Using food stamps at the store*
> *I didn't know what to wear*
> *Waiting in line for welfare*
>
> *If I wear my Anne Klein*
> *I will surely be denied*
> *If I take my Coach bag*
> *They might think I'm trying to brag*
> *If I wear my Farragamo shoes*
> *They won't believe I don't have food*
> *How did it get to this?*
>
> *I'm lonely po' an' sad*
> *My credit's really bad*
> *I didn't know what to wear*
> *Waiting in line for welfare*

I heard the roar of the applause. I thanked everyone, and as I was making my way back to my seat, people started coming over to me. Some of the people were thanking me for a wonderful presentation. But most of the others were handing me business cards and asking me for my card. "What are your speaking fees?" My speaking fees—I still hadn't figured that out yet. I was going to have to learn how to charge and what to charge.

By the afternoon, I'd made a lot of new friends. Later in the evening I was invited to join a group who was going to the hotel restaurant to eat. I froze. I had no money. I didn't want to reveal that I had no money, but at the same time I didn't want to seem like I wasn't interested in getting to know all of these wonderful people.

I decided I would just have an orange juice or something and pretend I wasn't hungry. I sat next to a woman named Gayle Bluebird. How does one describe Gayle Bluebird? Well, for starters, she is a mental health consumer advocate and activist. She's open, friendly, and I guess what I admire about her is she is definitely someone who makes up her own rules. From fashion to different ways to be an advocate for people with mental illness, Gayle follows her own heart.

Gayle wasn't buying the, "I'll just have orange juice. I'm not hungry" bit.

"Are they paying for your room?" She was so casual about it.

"What?"

"NAMI. Are they paying for your room?"

"Yes."

"Then sign the meal charges to your room."

"They didn't say I could do that."

She proceeded to tell me what was good and what was not so good on the menu. I don't remember what I ordered. But I remember enjoying it. When the check came, I charged the food to my room. I thought, "Life is good." The money I was expecting showed up in my account the next morning. I was able to get cash from the ATM for the rest of my trip. Many of the people I met at that conference I would see at other conferences and shows in the near future. Many of them I still consider either friends or cherished acquaintances.

We Will Not Fail

At the end of the summer, I drove to New Jersey to pick up Julie. When I arrived at Tony's house, it was as if a funeral was happening. Everybody was so sad. I tried to keep my excitement toned down. I didn't want anyone to have any reason to think I might still be crazy. I decided not to speak unless spoken to. We got Julie's things in the car. Marie was out of town visiting a college she was interested in attending after graduation. Tony and his girlfriend said some cheerless goodbyes and then Julie and I drove off. About three blocks away Julie and I were laughing and crying at the same time. We were so happy.

It seemed her father and most of my relatives were prepared for this reunion and adventure to fail. When we arrived at my apartment, Julie said something I will never, ever forget. She was aware of all the progress I'd made, but she was also aware that sometimes I still struggled financially. She also realized we weren't going to be able to count on anyone too much for support. If we seemed too needy, I'd be told I wasn't ready to handle the responsibility and Julie would probably be forced to go back. Julie, my miracle baby, took me by the hands, looked in my eyes and said, "We will not fail!" I hugged her, and we both cried.

I was starting to get more requests to speak or to do *Balancing Act* or *I Am Domestic Violence*. I bought books and searched the Internet to find out as much as I could about contracts and how to charge a fair fee for an engagement. I realized I was not the one to discuss money with potential clients. First of all, I was a pushover. I identified too closely with the consumers and victims. I'd hear how badly a group of people needed to hear what I had to say, or see my show, and I'd end up almost paying *them*.

I needed a manager, a booking agent, or somebody to at least negotiate and handle the contracts and yell at the clients who did everything but the things they agreed to do when they signed the contract.

I was so bogged down with getting paperwork done I considered closing down the performing business for a while. I was making money but not enough to hire assistants.

When I needed a box or stool for my show and I couldn't find the size that I preferred, I went to Home Depot, got some wood, and built the box in my living room. Based on what Kerry Nesbit had taught me about web design software, I started building and maintaining my own websites. I taught myself how to edit videos on my computer. I got some lights, and using a camera's self timer was able to do photos of myself that no one ever knew were not taken by a professional—or at least taken by someone else. I was taking the show and speaking inquiry calls, sending out promotional material, typing and mailing the contracts, hiring—and firing musicians, and ironing and maintaining the costumes for the shows.

I taught myself to braid extensions into my hair and to do my own make-up for my photos and for the shows. It was all fun and exciting, however, I was tired. I did all this so that I could savor those 35 to 70 minutes (depending on the presentation) that I got to be on stage. At one show, the show had started and I didn't know it. I was putting on make-up in the bathroom when my pianist came down and said, "They introduced you about 5 minutes ago."

When her school schedule allowed it, Julie traveled with me. She was my first official business and show assistant. We had some great times. As for the people waiting for us to fail—they started to understand it was not going to happen. Tony and Marie started visiting us more frequently. My mother and brothers were supportive. Roberta was still living in New York and seemed really happy that Julie was back with me.

Are We On Candid Camera?

Julie auditioned for, and was accepted into the North Carolina School of the Arts, School of Dance. She was super excited! I was super excited! We were both super excited! She would complete 11th and 12th grades there. The school was in Winston-Salem, about forty minutes from where we lived in Greensboro. She qualified for grants and would live on campus while studying there.

After the acceptance letter, we waited anxiously for the detailed information packet the acceptance letter said would soon come for us. After a few weeks, I called the admissions office to let them know I never received the other information. I was put on hold. When the woman returned, she said there had been a mistake and that Julie had *not* been accepted into the school.

I asked how they could make a mistake like that and how come I wasn't notified if there was a problem. I was put on hold again. "We don't remember your daughter's audition."

Was I on candid camera? "We don't remember your daughter's audition." *Is that was she said? I'm sure I misunderstood her.*

"Did you say you don't 'remember' my daughter's audition?"

Someone else came to the phone. "Why don't we bring Julie into our summer program where we can observe her and we will make a decision after that." It was obvious they were playing some game with me and my child. "Summer program? Okay. Fine. Put her in the summer program."

"Now, you do know the fee for the summer program is $2500."

"Wait, you expect me to pay for the summer program? You messed up and I'm supposed to pay you so you can observe my child over the summer and then decide whether or not she qualifies to be in your school. No. They can cast a Broadway show in a day. It's going to cost me $2500 and a whole summer for you to decide if my daughter can study at your school? No. Let me speak to somebody who can tell me what is really going on here."

By now I haven't a clue who I'm speaking to. I asked to speak to the dean. *Of course deans are always in meetings.* I spoke to various people who held various positions at the school over the next few days. No one knew anything or had the power to do anything—or, so they said.

All of Julie's dance teachers agreed that students with far less technique, talent and dedication had been accepted into the school for the coming year. The best the school would offer was a new audition date. By now both Julie and I knew something fishy was going on. I took Julie back to Winston-Salem for her second audition. They put Julie in a class of college seniors to dance with them and do routines that they'd worked on for a whole semester. *This would be her audition?* She was being set up.

I told her to go in there and have a good time. When the class started she went in. I sat outside by the door. When the class was over, she didn't come out right away. I was concerned and I went in. The other students and the teacher were telling her what a great job she did. When the woman who had arranged the audition came back, Julie and I were all smiles. She spoke briefly with the teacher and then she said to me, "I would like to observe her over the summer."

When we got back home I wrote a letter to the governor, the mayor of Winston-Salem, some local politicians, and a few members of the North Carolina General Assembly I'd met while performing some of my shows. I explained the details of the situation. The North Carolina School of the Arts is a public school. I didn't feel I should have to pay $2500 in order to know whether Julie was accepted into their program—especially since I was already holding in my hands an official letter from the school that clearly states my daughter was already accepted into the school. Most of the people I wrote letters to responded and said they would look into the matter.

Within two weeks, we received a new acceptance letter with all of the detailed information. However, the letter they sent to Julie was worded in a way that implied they *had* to accept her—they actually managed to work in the word "obliged". There was no, "we're happy", "we're sorry about the mix-up", "we're glad you're here"—none of that. There was something cold and unkind and uncaring about the whole situation.

Julie and I decided to move back to New York City. We both wanted to stretch our creative wings. What place is better for that than the 'Big Apple?' I felt ready to go back. The only reason I had come back to Greensboro was I was sick and broke with two small children. Julie and I both longed for the city again.

We initially moved in with my sister who owns a house in Harlem. The house was still being renovated, so even though it was a big house, only one floor was inhabitable. So, basically, the three of us lived in a one-bedroom apartment. My sister slept in the living room, and Julie and I slept in the bedroom. I was constantly apartment-hunting. Marie had just graduated from high school and was going to college in California.

Synchronicity

In January of 2000 I turned 50 years old. I felt—well, in a word—happy. I was enjoying my life and finally, I was enjoying being me. In between my show gigs, I worked as a temp through a really fine employment/temporary agency in New York. I mostly worked as a receptionist for various companies and organizations in the city. As a temp I experienced lots of different settings and all kinds of people. Sometimes I would literally work at five different companies in one week. Now that I was feeling good about myself, I enjoyed studying human nature and how other people dealt with their life obstacles.

One of the most intriguing things to me was how people could see other people but, not acknowledge them. For instance, usually as the receptionist, I was the very first person you saw when you entered the office. I was front and center. No way to miss me. Yet, when the employees came to work in the mornings—and even after I pushed the button that allowed the door to open for them, they'd just walk right past me like I wasn't there. This amused me. If I spoke to them, they would respond, however, if I didn't say anything, most of them just pretended like I was invisible. I used to make a game of saying, "Good morning! How are you today?" in a real bouncy, friendly voice, just to see what their reaction would be. This amused me. It annoyed them. Everyone wasn't like this, but a good number of people were.

I worked for some non-profits that for the life of me I couldn't figure out what it was they did. I encountered CEOs with walls of photos of them with starving Third World children who they were vowing to save: Yet again; I was invisible to them until they needed something. (And they called me crazy.)

I was invited to do several presentations of *I Am Domestic Violence* in Brevard, NC in June of 2000. The first performance was at a Sunday morning church service. Before the program started, I was sitting with the congregation. The elderly couple I sat next to, and I, started a conversation. Even though I was trying to be discreet about the fact that I was going to perform, they told me they recognized my picture from the local paper.

Carroll and Lucy Teeter were newly weds who lived in Florida, but were spending time at their mountain home in Brevard. After my performance, the Teeters told me they were associated with Habitat for Humanity in Winter Haven, Florida. They were having a special Habitat event and wondered if, for their event, I could create a show that showed how Habitat for Humanity changed people's lives.

We made arrangements for me to entertain and present the show about Habitat changing lives at the

Florida event. When I went online to gather information about Habitat for my show, I was surprised to see that Habitat for Humanity had an affiliate in New York City. I'd always thought of Habitat as a rural program. I saw an online application and the requirements. I remember thinking, "Humm. I qualify for this". I filled out the application, submitted it, and promptly forgot about it.

I went on with my research, put the show together, and traveled to Florida. The guest speakers at the event were the founders of Habitat for Humanity, Linda and Millard Fuller. I immediately like them. They were personable, down to earth, and easy to talk with, and both had a great sense of humor. Mrs. Fuller has spoken publicly about dealing with her own depression, and is an advocate for people with mental illnesses.

The Teeters were incredibly gracious hosts. Among other places, they took me to visit their orange grove. (I'd never been to an orange grove before.) They went all out to make me feel welcome and comfortable. As I am writing this, Mr. Teeter is about to celebrate his 90th birthday.

About a year after the Winter Haven event, I was pleasantly surprised and thrilled to receive two significant letters on the <u>exact</u> same day. One letter was from Mrs. Fuller inviting me to participate in a program at The Carter Center in Atlanta, Georgia, and do a presentation similar to what she'd seen in

Winter Haven on the correlation between homelessness and mental illness.

The second letter was from Habitat for Humanity – New York City informing me that I was next on the list to *own* a home—pending the outcome of additional paperwork and in-home interview. The condo was located in a building two blocks from where Julie and I lived with my sister. Since the building was nearly finished, we would have to complete our 600 hours of sweat equity (hours spent building a home in exchange for a down payment) by helping to build other Habitat homes in various areas of the city. I gathered the necessary documents for Habitat while I prepared the presentation for the Mental Health Partnership Steering Council 2002 Annual Meeting held at The Carter Center. I was extremely honored to have been a part of this event.

About a month later, I received two more unexpected, yet fantastic letters. The first letter was from Rosalynn Carter inviting me to do the presentation she saw at The Carter Center for her husband, former President Carter, during the Jimmy Carter Weekend. The second letter, which came the following day, was from Habitat – NYC, and it said I had been approved to be a homeowner. Julie and I were totally giddy. *Me, a homeowner? Was I dreaming? Incredible! Thank you God!* Right away, Julie and I started traveling to construction sites to complete our sweat equity hours. Even if it rained, we wouldn't leave. We'd ask for work that we could do in the rain.

I traveled to Americus, Georgia to attend the Jimmy Carter Weekend. It was extraordinary. I met people from all over the world, visited Habitat for Humanity International, laid a few cement blocks for a house in Global Village (life-size Habitat houses from countries around the world), helped build a house for a family, did my presentation at a dinner for President Carter, and attended a Sunday school class he taught at the Maranatha Baptist Church in Plains, Georgia.

When I got back to New York, Julie and I did construction on homes in Manhattan, Brooklyn, Queens and the Bronx. Marie, Tony and JoJo came on a few occasions to help. We finished our sweat equity in record time. We moved into our new home on the hottest day in June 2002. The first night we only had what each of us could bring in a small box. We smiled all night.

I understand the word synchronicity to mean divine coincidences of unrelated things that are all part of a bigger picture. This is a word I would use to explain how I became a homeowner in New York City. Yeah. Synchronicity.

Wet and Wavy

I'd only been back in New York a few months when, in addition to the Brevard and Winter Haven invitations, I received a call from the Tennessee NAMI. They were interested in booking *Balancing Act*. They told me they would like to present it in Nashville at the Ryman Auditorium—the original Grand Ole Opry. "Oh my God. That's really big time!" I thought. They wanted me to come and bring three musicians.

Before the show, I was invited to come to Nashville to do publicity for the upcoming show. The evening before I was to leave, I decided to braid extensions into my hair. I'd finished about three-quarters of my head when I discovered I didn't have enough hair to finish the job. I went to bed and got up really early to go get the hair at the beauty supply store near me. I went to the ATM. "What!" I almost fainted. It said my account had been frozen. I ran home and called the bank. Surely, this is a mistake. I talked to someone at the bank. I was trying my best to remain calm.

The bank officer said, "The last two statements we sent you were returned to us. For security reasons, we have to freeze the account until we can verify the address"

"I can verify the address right now."

"Well, we are going to send you a form in the mail and you have 10 days to respond. It is the only way we can verify that you still live at that address." I could share the rest of the conversation with you. But what it boiled down to was I was not getting any money that day. That's why having several bank accounts can be a good thing. Well, here I was supposed to fly to Nashville in a few hours and I didn't have a full weave or any cash.

One of the things that I'd brought with me when I moved in with Roberta was a double VCR machine that I used for making publicity videos for my shows. It had a slot for two video cassettes and made copies of videos very easily. I had packed it back in its original box when we made the move. I put the VCR in our rolling cart (used to take clothes to the laundromat) and rolled my VCR three blocks to the beauty supply store. The owner was a young African man. I said, "Do you remember me? I was here yesterday?"

"Oh yes", he said.

"Well I need another pack of this hair. I need two to be sure that I have enough this time," I said, pointing to the hair on my head.

"Oh. Yes, 'wet and wavy'." He smiled and pulled out two packs from underneath the counter. "Fifteen dollars."

"I have a situation," I said, "I have to go out of town today and I won't have any money until I get back in four days. This is a fabulous VCR. It really works great. I want you to hold it here until I come back from Tennessee."

He just looked at the box for a while.

"You can take it out of the box and plug it in. It really works. I need the hair today. Give me the hair and you keep the VCR until I come back with the fifteen dollars."

I left the store with 2 packs of wet and wavy #4, borrowed $100 from Luther, went home and finished my hair and then flew to Nashville.

Thank You

For most of the North Carolina tour of *Balancing Act*, I worked with a very talented pianist who lived in Greensboro. We got along well and she was always professional. A couple of times she'd brought her husband and toddler son with her when we went places that required an overnight stay. She was the first person I thought of when I was hiring musicians for the Nashville show. My bass player, Kenneth Hawkins, and drummer, Melvin McClean, also lived in Greensboro.

Of course, NAMI was paying for all of our travel expenses. Kenneth and Melvin would be bringing instruments and some sound equipment, so they wanted to rent a van and drive. Since the pianist wouldn't be traveling with an instrument and she was the only female, they offered to buy her an airline ticket.

She'd just had a new baby and didn't want to leave the baby because she was nursing. Therefore, she wanted to bring her husband to watch the baby when she was busy with the show. In other words, the whole family would come to Nashville. No one had a problem with that. Where we hit a snag was when she wanted me or NAMI to pay for all of their tickets. I explained only one ticket would be paid for by NAMI.

Okay. She sees a good deal on airline tickets and buys the tickets for her family. Then, NAMI changes the date of the show. She can't get her money back for the tickets and wants me or NAMI to reimburse her. This was a big problem. All I knew to do was to say as nicely as I knew how, "No."

The situation became severe when she took it upon herself to call NAMI (without my knowledge) asking to be reimbursed for the tickets. She was working for me. For her to call the sponsor directly—well, in a different situation I could have lost the gig. NAMI reimbursed her half of her money, but told me they didn't want her to play the show. I reimbursed the other half in order to put closure on this and move on. However, I never worked with her again. NAMI got one of Nashville's finest musicians, John Hobbs, a songwriter, producer, and keyboardist to be musical director and pianist for the show.

Although I tried to sleep until later, I woke up at the crack of dawn on October 22, 2000. The show was scheduled to start at seven that evening. I opened the curtains and looked out the hotel window. Downtown Nashville was still asleep. I went to the closet to check that my *Balancing Act* costume, the maroon jumpsuit and dyed to match shoes, were still there. I sat on the bed with my legs crossed Indian Style. I meditated for about an hour. I thanked God for all of these wonderful things that were happening for me. I thanked God in advance for a fabulous and successful show. I laid down on the bed with my eyes closed and rehearsed the whole show in my head. I'd rehearsed the night before with the musical director. That was a blast.

I was eager to walk on the Ryman stage, so I was happy to see Melissa, who was working with NAMI, when she came to take me over to the theater. It was beautiful there. I felt beautiful there. The musicians had been set up on one side of the stage. Down front and center was my box. I got dressed in my show outfit and the theater technicians got me hooked up with a wireless body microphone and we did a sound check.

It wasn't long before Dixie Gamble was welcoming the audience. She also spoke about her connection to the mental health community and why NAMI was important. As I stood in the wings that night, I felt like there was magic in the air. When Joyce Judge, NAMI Tennessee's executive director, introduced me, butterflies leaped around in my stomach for a couple of seconds.

The overture started. Then I heard the piano chimes. The chords to the *Balancing Act* prologue song that invited me on stage. I walked on stage and joined my box down front and center. There I was just me and my box on the stage of the original Grand Ole Opry. The chords continued until I was ready. I looked out and around the audience. I smiled and then I sang:

> *Once upon a time and long long ago*
> *When I heard bedtime stories that's how they used to go*
> *Though the tales would always lull me to sleep*
> *I realize those stories were not so unique*
> *For there's one thing that I've learned*
> *And I've learned quite well*
> *That is everybody has a story to tell*

I then segued into the first scene. The scenes rolled in and out of one another smoothly. Like my real life, some scenes were frantic and others were calm. There were funny lines and also the lines that brought tears to eyes. Most of the vignettes were ultimately punctuated with a song. "I Forgot," closed the show on an optimistic note. I had a ball on stage and all too soon the show was over. The audience gave a moving, standing ovation.

"Thank you! Thank you!" I took another bow. Mrs. Judge brought me a bouquet of flowers. I was in the spot light on the very stage so many internationally renowned artists had graced. I was alive. People were clapping for me. When I think of how close I came to ending my life . . . "Thank you!" I smiled at the audience and said, "Thank you!"

Epilogue

That's my story—as much of it as I could fit in this book. Of course, this is not the *end* of my story. So very much has happened in the last nine years and my adventurous journey continues. However, here is where I will end the story for now.

Marie graduated from Hunter College with a dance degree, lives with her musician husband in Washington Heights, loves to travel and is becoming quite a savvy business woman.

Julie graduated from New York City College with a music degree and is now in Hollywood. She works at a yoga studio, enjoys her lunches on the beach, and is moving forward with her acting career. My children are my biggest fans and supporters and I am theirs.

Their father and I are friends. At least we were before this book was published. He loves his daughters as much as I do. Today, he is there for them in every sense of the word.

My mother is dealing with the later stages of Alzheimer's and lives with my sister in New York. My mother does not recognize me or remember me as her daughter.

One of my proudest moments was witnessing my sister, Roberta, receive her Fellowship medal during the Investiture of Fellows Ceremony at the American Institute of Architects (AIA) 2006 National Convention and Design Expo in Los Angeles. Tears filled my eyes when her name was called. I was reminded of how many people tried to convince my sister that becoming a black female architect was not a realistic dream. Out of a total AIA membership of nearly 78,000, there are fewer than 3,000 distinguished with the honor of fellowship.

My brothers Joel and Justin both still live in Greensboro. I have love and respect for them because they are fine, respectable and loving men. I'm happy they are my brothers. Joel is married, is a fine chef and works in the food industry. The baby, Justin, is married, has two daughters the same ages as Marie and Julie and he recently became a grandfather. After retiring from the Navy, he started working with the local Sheriff's Department. He is always ready for the next incredible life adventure.

I currently live in New York City. I enjoy speaking and entertaining. I love learning and sharing information about human potential—our innate intelligence, strength and creativity. I also enjoy doing absolutely nothing. I stopped trying to make everything make sense. I don't take any medication and prefer natural alternatives and home remedies. I'm thinking about starting a new career as a standup comedienne, or perhaps a rhythm and blues singer or a combination of the two.

My Aunt Thelma, my mother's sister, is 95 years young. She was diagnosed with colon cancer about five years ago. She refused to have surgery and all other invasive medical treatment. According to all of her medical documentation, she should have died a few years ago. However, she still lives alone in the senior citizen complex, flirts with the roadside vegetable sellers, can walk faster than I can, and is teaching me an invaluable lesson about living and dying on your own terms.

These Feet Need to be Dancing

These feet have marched for freedom

These feet have walked for a cure

These feet have run for my life

These feet have stood on principle

And waited on a promise

These feet have walked through fire

And climbed stairs constructed only of faith

These feet need to be DANCING! - Wambu

PART TWO - Lessons I Learned Along the Way

Now that I've opened the door to my life, I'd like to invite you to have a front-row seat as I share some of the strategies, techniques, information and resources that were vital to my transformation from a tired, angry, guilty, scared, ashamed and suicidal person to a person of joy, happiness, peace, love and enthusiasm for life.

As I stated in the introduction: I know there are people with developmental issues and others who may have suffered a physical trauma that may not allow them to take full charge of their lives at this time. However, if you can read the words in this book and comprehend them, then I believe you can recover and heal your life—mind, body, soul and spirit. You have the power to rise above (I did not say cure) whatever mental physical or emotional challenges you have, and have a joyful, peaceful and healthy life.

Reclaiming your life will involve:

* * * Developing a new positive perspective on life in general.

* * * Learning to love and accept yourself and know that it is all right to do so.

* * * Understanding that what you put in and on your body does effect, not only your physical body, but your mind, emotions and spirit.

* * * Checking for toxic culprits in your environment that may be effecting you negatively. This includes people.

* * * Deciding what and how you want to be.

* * * Forgiving yourself and everyone who you feel has ever hurt you in any way.

* * * Developing an attitude of gratitude.

* * * Questioning everything. Don't just believe something because everybody else says it's so.

On the following pages I share some of the lessons I learned along the way.

It's an Ongoing Process

"People often say that motivation doesn't last. Well, neither does bathing—that's why we recommend it daily." - Zig Ziglar

Some of the most expensive musical instruments in the world include the Lady Tennant Stradivari violin, which is valued at over $2.03 million and John Lennon's Steinway piano, which is valued at over $1.03 million. What do these valued instruments have in common with you? It doesn't matter how precious they are, if they are not tuned on a regular basis, they will sound lousy.

If you do not tune-up yourself on a regular basis you will not only sound lousy, you will look lousy, and feel lousy. Taking care of ourselves is not a one shot deal. It's not a one week or one month or one year deal. It is an ongoing process that hopefully is thrilling and fun.

Know Your Value

*"You know the value of every merchandise, but
you do not know your own value . . ."*
-The Spiritual Teachings of Rumi

All of my challenges stemmed from one basic
truth. I had no sense of my own self-worth. I was
busy trying to be liked, not cause problems, get into
heaven, follow the rules and do what, I thought, was
expected of me. I was on auto-pilot and not really
living; just moving and constantly reacting to every-
one and everything around me.

I was settling for whatever came my way with-
out a thought that I could plan my life better and
decide exactly what I wanted. There is a saying, "If
you fail to plan, you plan to fail." That is exactly what
I did. I failed to plan. As a result, I was powerless.
Undeniably the most blatant testament to my sense
of worthlessness was when I allowed someone to not
only verbally abuse me, but to physically abuse me as
well.

There are hundreds of men and women who are
caught up in abusive situations and are suffering in
silence as I did. I do not know how to keep ruthless
people from doing terrible things. However, I do know

it is impossible to move in a positive direction if we can't honor and love ourselves. It is up to each of us to understand and appreciate our worth and not allow another human to decide our value.

I'm sure you've heard people refer to babies as miracles. I've heard some say, "Babies are such a blessing—a precious gift from God." We all started out as babies. We do not stop being a miracle or precious gift from God just because we get older or bigger or are diagnosed with a so-called disease. We are still miracles!

Other people will unconsciously take their clues from you and treat you the way you treat yourself. Be honest, do you care for your clothes or your car better than you care for yourself? It is easy to believe the barrage of media messages that say we're not attractive enough or perhaps we are too tall, too short, too thin, too fat, too young, too old, too dark, too light, too poor and even—too rich.

In fact, our whole economic system is based on keeping us—the public—feeling 'less than'—believing there is something wrong with us—and then we are presented with an array of products that promise to make us whole and more acceptable. Before they can sell us that jar of beauty cream, they must first sell us the idea that we look bad and will be unhappy without it.

The first audio tape program I ordered was filled with messages about the strength and innate wisdom that each of us is born with. I was reminded that I had the power to create my own life rules and decide for myself who and what I want to be and how I want to live.

I made a conscious choice to feel good and to fill my life with good people and good things—people and things that please me, support me, and allow me to express myself in positive ways.

I've spent years getting bad things out of my life and good things into my life. But it all started with a commitment to do it! You have to want to improve your life. Surrounding myself with inspirational words and encouragement was a wonderful first step because I was constantly reminded that I could rise above almost any challenge. My favorite quote, and the one that hangs on my bedroom wall today is, *"It's never too late to be what you might have been."* - George Eliot

Establish a Spiritual Relationship

"People see God every day, they just don't recognize Him." - Pearl Bailey

During some of my psychotic episodes (for instance, that unexpected California trip), I could not remember what I was supposed to be doing. My mind slipped in and our of reality. I would go days without eating and without sleeping.

Nevertheless, through it all, my heart kept beating. The blood kept circulating through my veins, and my lungs continued to do what lungs do to keep you breathing. Who was doing that? I had no clue how to keep my heart beating. Yet, it kept beating.

Some power greater than myself was at work. Who or what had told my cells where they needed to be and what they needed to do? I was not controlling these things. We are all alive and well today because there is something bigger than our human selves, something bigger than our human doctors, that is in charge. I have come to refer to that thing—that power, as God or the Universe.

Call this powerful entity whatever you wish. Some call it God, The Universe or Creator, Divine, Lord, Allah, Jehovah, Yahweh, Ra, Almighty, Heavenly Father or Mother Nature. Some have other names for it or him or her. Still others have no name for it.

Let's not debate about names or gender. It does not matter what you call it, as long as you acknowledge the mighty force that is around us, in us, and is us.

We are true expressions of God. I heard someone liken it to dipping a glass in the ocean. If you were to take a glass down to the ocean, dip the glass in the ocean and fill the glass with water from the ocean, what would you have in the glass? You would not have the whole ocean in the glass, but everything the ocean is—the essence of the ocean—would be in the glass. Our relationship with God is the same. We are the essence of God.

The same magic that runs through butterflies and hummingbirds and snowflakes and rain runs through us. We have the same power those creations have that can only be described as wonderful, miraculous and phenomenal. We are wonderful, miraculous and phenomenal. Each of us owns that power that no scientist and no doctor have ever been able to capture and put in a bell jar. That *power* is the essence of who we are—our spirit—our Godness—our All-that-ness.

For years I was angry at God for allowing bad things to happen to me. I was also angry with God for being a vengeful God. Was God punishing me? I now understand I had a wrong idea of who and what God was. Then I got clear that God is pure love energy. The God I feared as a child was a man-made interpretation of God. A God who would punish me or make me feel ashamed or have me beg for forgiveness—or *beg* for anything was not *my* God.

I now have an extraordinary relationship with a loving God—a God who honors and serves me, as I in turn, honor and serve her.

Turn the TV Off

"Today's audience knows more about what's on television than what's in life." - Larry Gelbart

Take a break from media overload. Turn the TV off and do not read the newspapers. I learned many years ago not to watch the news. As a person who suffered from depression for many years, I learned that watching the news did not agree with me—especially just before going to bed.

Those news stories stay with you in your sub-conscious. Let's face it: Except for a warm and fuzzy human-interest story now and then, the news is not good. You will find yourself listening to sad stories and pondering devastating events you can do nothing about. The old saying, "No news is good news" is true.

Knowing who was voted out of the house on a reality TV show really is not going to affect our lives unless we are that person who was voted off, or we are somehow personally connected to that person. We spend time thinking about and discussing movie characters, answers to game shows, other people's business, and what's wrong or right about our political system.

True, we are not hurting anybody, and yes, there are worse things we could be doing. However, we are not really helping ourselves either. Imagine if we spent this time thinking and planning our own lives—thinking about ways to make our own lives better, and thinking about things that we want to have, to be, and to do.

I haven't had a TV for years and I don't even miss it. My home feels more peaceful and I get a lot more done each day. Even on the internet I stay clear of the news and gossip sites. I will admit that when I'm in someone's home that has a TV, I become mesmerized by it. It is as if I've never seen a TV before. This behavior, of course, only confirms why I don't need one in my own home.

For a wonderful, healthy and pleasurable experience, I challenge you and your family to take a TV fast. TV addiction is real, and many people have difficulty breaking the TV habit. Your eyes, your brain, your ears, and your whole body will thank you. Take back your mind and your life. Deprogram!

"Forgiveness does not change the past, but it does enlarge the future."
-Paul Boese

A major hurdle I faced was forgiving myself. I was angry at myself for not being mentally stronger and smarter. I was embarrassed about some of my behavior. I felt I had caused my children to suffer unnecessarily. Sometimes when I felt good, I thought I had no right to feel good. I felt guilty about not feeling guilty.

We can choose to forgive ourselves at any time. Just say, "I forgive me." You don't even have to say it out loud—just think it. Yes, it is that easy.

Each of us has the power to forgive ourselves as many times as we need to. Let's learn from our mistakes, try to do the right thing and move on. Know that it is alright to forgive yourself. It is alright to love yourself. No one can accomplish anything feeling guilty, shameful or angry.

Harboring hurt feelings and being upset over something someone did or did not do is *not* affecting them. You are only ruining your own happiness and health. Do not allow someone who has already hurt you to have a starring role in your life.

Every time you think about them or tell the tale of how they hurt you, you are turning your spotlight on them. Get them off your life stage. Forgive them. Write them out of your life script.

Eat Life-Giving Foods

"As our body machine runs entirely upon the energy or 'strength' which it gets out of its food, a good food must have plenty of fuel value . . ."
- Woods Hutchinson, A. M., M. D.

After I made a commitment to take charge of taking care of me, I looked at what I was eating. I was understanding the association between how food not only affects our physical body, but how what we eat affects our mental or emotional and spiritual well being.

If you eat devitalized and lifeless food, it makes sense you will be devitalized and lifeless. Your body has nothing on which to draw to keep it energetic and vibrant. If you do not feel like cooking, then eat apples or other fruits or vegetables.

You do not have to have a full plate of a variety of food in order to have a good meal. Even though you may crave sugar and junk food, these foods not only do not help in relieving depression and other negative symptoms, they make them worse.

I read a book called *Sugar Blues* by William Duffy. Among other things, this book talks about the link between sugar and depression, and the author even goes so far as to suggest that eliminating refined sugar from the diet of those institutionalized for mental illness could be an effective treatment for some. I eliminated sugar from my diet and I did find that I was more energetic and less moody.

I eventually eliminated white bread and dairy products as well. I stopped eating white bread because I noticed I was always sleepy after eating it. Besides knowing that milk products are hard to digest for some people, I stopped dairy because—well, think about it—we are the only species that drink the milk of another species—the milk that was intended for their babies.

The time I felt the most vibrant, clean, healthy and alert were the three months I was 100% raw. A raw food diet or lifestyle is the consumption of only unprocessed and uncooked plant foods—nuts, seeds, vegetables and fruits. It's a lot more interesting and fun than it sounds. I invite you to at least investigate it.

Buy and eat organic foods, if possible. It has not been determined how chemically treated and Genetically Modified (GM) foods, more accurately called genetically engineered foods and other additives affect us, so best to avoid them. Genetically modified foods are foods that have had their DNA altered through genetic engineering.

A nutritionist told me if I couldn't pronounce what was in a product, don't eat the product. I still follow that rule today—as closely as I can. I started learning about fasting and have done several fasts over the past few years. Whenever I start to feel poorly, a short fast and a colon cleanse does wonders for me. I feel better right away.

Ultimately, you should do and eat what feels right and good to, and for you. There is no one food or one way of eating that will serve us all equally. I do encourage you, however, to explore all the possibilities. Understand that the food we eat does matter, and can make a difference in whether we feel well or feel sick.

"Old people shouldn't eat health foods. They need all the preservatives they can get."
- Robert Orben

Stop Trying To Please Everybody

"I don't know the key to success, but the key to failure is trying to please everybody." - Bill Cosby

Trying to please other people is a sure prescription for unhappiness and personal pain. You will never be able to please everyone. The best you can do is to be true to yourself. Do what makes you feel good. Follow your intuition.

If you do "A", there will always be someone who says, you should have done "B" and of course, if you do "B", there will be those who are upset with you because you didn't do "A."

Usually the people who are the most disturbed with your decisions, or concerned with what you are doing, are the ones who are miserable themselves, or they would be too busy enjoying their lives to care what you are doing with yours.

I spent a lot of the years trying to please people. I didn't want anyone to be angry with me. I didn't want anyone to say anything bad about me. I didn't know how to say, "No." This was a very stressful and unfulfilling way to live.

Today if I find myself in a dilemma, I try to work it out so that everyone involved is happy with

the outcome. However, sometimes, I have to let who-
ever is going to be angry or unhappy with a decision I
make, be angry or unhappy. I often recall a book I
read by Dr. Terry Cole-Whittaker entitled *What You
Think of Me is None of My Business*. I think the title
says it all.

"If you can laugh at it, you can live with it."
- Erma Bombeck

Norman Cousins is often described as the man who laughed himself back to health. According to his autobiography, Norman Cousins—a prominent political journalist, author, professor, and world peace advocate—was diagnosed with ankylosing spondylitis, a painful spine condition. He put himself on large doses of vitamin C and humor—which included watching a lot of Marks Brothers' movies.

He says, "I made the joyous discovery that ten minutes of genuine belly laughter had an anesthetic effect and would give me at least two hours of pain-free sleep. When the pain-killing effect of the laughter wore off, we would switch on the motion picture projector again, and not infrequently, it would lead to another pain-free interval."

We all know how good it feels to laugh. Have you ever "laughed 'til it hurts?" Well, perhaps that's a sign that those laughing muscles are not used often enough. Whenever possible and appropriate, laugh. Don't laugh at the expense of someone else's feelings. A healthy laugh requires a healthy attitude. A hearty laugh should embrace those around you, not alienate them.

I love to laugh. Whenever I'm feeling down, I just start smiling. There is no way you can feel bad, sad or depressed if you force yourself to smile and laugh. Try it! Yeah, right now. Doesn't that feel great?

Drs. Gael Crystal and Patrick Flanagan, authors of the article entitled *Laughter—Still the Best Medicine* (1995), say, "Laughter is a form of internal jogging that exercises the body and stimulates the release of beneficial brain neurotransmitters and hormones. Positive outlook and laughter is actually good for our health!"

Try to see the humor in day to day situations you might find yourself in. Don't be overly sensitive to what someone says or to another person's point of view.

So, how many psychiatrists does it take to change a light bulb? Only one—but it will take a long, long time, and the light bulb has got to really want to change. - Unknown

Meditate

" . . . act the part of the wise man, and go each day into the silence, there commune with the Infinite, there dwell for a season with the Infinite Spirit of all life, of all power; for you can get true power in no other way." - Ralph Waldo Trine

Meditation is the act of focusing our thoughts away from the physical world. Meditation is the calming of our body and our mind in order to connect more deeply with our God source—our wisdom, our intuition and our power. Meditation refreshes the spirit, mind and body.

Meditation is free. It does not cost anything to sit quietly and focus your thoughts. However, for many of us, quieting our minds, focusing away from our challenges, or even relaxing, is "easier said than done."

Teaching myself to meditate has been one of the best gifts I have ever given myself. Meditation also provides physical and mental benefits as well. Some of the benefits include:

        * * * General better health

        * * * Lower blood pressure

        * * * Better energy

        * * * Maintaining a youthful vitality

        * * * Better concentration

        * * * The ability to relax and to feel peaceful

Today, many researchers and medical authorities also believe that meditation can help:

  * * * Relieve fatigue and sleep disorders

  * * * Increase one's IQ

  * * * Relieve anxiety

  * * * Decrease depression

  * * * Decrease irritability and moodiness

  * * * Improve learning ability and memory

  * * * Increase happiness

I spend an hour a day meditating when I first wake up in the mornings. However, you can spend as little as a half hour a day and receive great benefits. You will find that even fifteen minutes of meditation can make you feel relaxed and refreshed before, during, or after a busy day.

If you would like some guidance, there are plenty of excellent meditation CDs, videos and books in stores and on the Internet. The most important thing you need in order to meditate is your wonderful, beautiful, magnificent self and the sincere intention to calm, relax and rejuvenate your mind, body, and spirit.

Investigate Energy Healing

"According to theories of traditional Chinese medicine (TCM), illness is mainly the result of an imbalance in the flow of ch'i energy to the organs of the body." - Richard Gerber, M.D.

Three examples of energy healing methods are reiki, acupuncture, EFT or Emotional Freedom Techniques. There are many others. I only mention these three because these are three that I have experienced and found helpful at one time or another for my children and me.

Some forms of chanting, singing and dancing are also considered to be energy balancing practices. However, the method that I'm most familiar with and use on a daily basis is EFT or Emotional Freedom Techniques.

In school, I learned about the many systems of our bodies—including the digestive system, the respiratory system, the nervous system, and the skeletal system. However, I do not recall hearing much about our energy system.

Although we cannot see our subtle energy fields, these vital forces can give us access to great wisdom, intuition, and perfect health. Without our life energy system, we are just mechanical bodies.

A glitch or malfunction in our energy system is just as serious as a malfunction in our digestive, nervous, or any other system in our body. However, when we are looking for relief from our physical and emotional challenges, we often fail to check our energy system to make sure it is balanced and in proper working order.

I was so fascinated with these techniques that I became an EFT practitioner. Emotional Freedom Techniques (EFT) are the easiest, fastest and most cost-effective way I know to balance and align our energy system. It's easy to learn, simple to use and, like meditation, all you need is you.

According to Gary Craig, who is credited with being the founder of EFT, "The cause of all negative emotions is a disruption in the body's energy system. This common sense approach draws its power from:

(1) Time-honored Eastern discoveries that have been around for over 5,000 years and

(2) Albert Einstein, who told us back in the 1920s that everything (including our bodies) is composed of energy.

These ideas have been largely ignored by Western Healing Practices and that is why EFT often works where nothing else will. It's not that EFT is so stunning (although it may certainly appear that way to you). Rather, it is because conventional healing methods have simply overlooked the obvious."

Today, many doctors, including psychiatrists, use EFT in their practices.

Explore Pure Essential Oils and Aromatherapy

"It's so nice to get flowers while you can still smell the fragrance." - Lena Horne

Aromatherapy, an alternative medicine that uses essential oils to enhance a person's health or mood, is an age-old practice. Aromatherapy is an ancient healing practice that has been used for upwards of 6000 years. Many different cultures, including the Greeks, Romans and ancient Egyptians used essential oils and aromatherapy.

Essential oils are mentioned 188 times in the Bible. Oils were used for anointing and to heal the sick. Some of the more popular oils were frankincense, myrrh, rosemary, hyssop and spikenard. In fact, it was frankincense and myrrh that the wise men brought as gifts to the Christ Child.

Today, aromatherapy is used by many people for a variety of ailments ranging from depression to poison ivy to the flu. Each oil has certain properties that work to treat specific conditions. There are special "blends" of various essential oils that combine to bring about a desired healing effect. These blends can be applied to the skin, used in a diffuser or sprayed into the air and then inhaled.

Many essential oils have strong antiseptic properties. They are often used to combat infection, and some are inhaled by people who are battling a cold or flu. Some essential oils are also believed to have strong effects on the mind and are used to uplift a person's mood. Likewise, other oils, such as lavender, are used for relaxation and to aid in sleep. Different essential oils offer different therapeutic benefits.

The pure essential oils are very concentrated and some can have adverse effects if not handled properly. Today, aromatherapy is recognized as a comprehensive natural therapy by many healthcare professionals. Keep in mind that, as with any product on the market, all essential oils are not created equal.

I usually carry bottles of oils with me all the time. I take a whiff of various oils when I encounter bad odors, or have a stuffy nose, or I want to feel refreshed.

For those who might doubt the power of aromas and the effect they have on us, I offer this excerpt from an article entitled U.S. Military Is Seeking Ultimate "Stink Bomb" by Bijal P. Trivedi, National Geographic Today, January 7, 2002.

"The task: to develop an odor so universally repulsive it would be considered unbearable by people from all cultures. That's the challenge the U.S. Department of Defense has presented to scientists at the

Monell Chemical Senses Center in Philadelphia, Pennsylvania.

The military wants to use the odor to control crowds and deter people from restricted areas, according to psychologist Pamela Dalton, who studies the development of odor preferences at Monell . . . The odors also induced increased heart rate and stomach uneasiness—early symptoms of nausea . . .

This hasn't happened yet, but it could if the US Army succeeds in its effort to create the mother of all stink bombs. Their aim is to have a weapon that doesn't kill or injure anyone, but instead triggers fear, panic and an overwhelming urge to run away. The mixture of malodorous molecules has to add up to a pong [stench] so repulsive it's truly terrifying."

I have to conclude that odors do have psychological and physical affects on us. If bad odors can cause fear and make the body feel sick, then, it seems to me that perhaps the odor of pure essential oils from nature's fragrant flowers would help me to feel uplifted and well.

"Lack of money is no obstacle. Lack of an idea is an obstacle." - Ken Hakuta

If you have been displaced, or if you are not working due to a mental illness or some other illness or challenge in your life, then you are in the right place to start your own business. This means finding that thing that you love to do and areas where you are talented and finding ways to make money from them.

Many times, because of the stigma surrounding mental illness, finding a job can be difficult. Even if your future employer doesn't know that you had a mental illness, they may still want you to account for those missing years on your resume. Due to lack of financial support or poor decisions we've made, our credit history may be less than perfect. Nowadays, many employers look at our credit reports to decide whether or not we're worthy of working for them.

So, if these things are working against you—the lost years, the credit report, not having a wardrobe to present at an office setting every day, or childcare issues, then consider being your own boss.

We have been led to believe that this is more difficult than it is. Study other people who are making money doing things that you are interested in. Use them as a role model and then research and study what needs to be done in order to make your dream of having your own business a reality.

I don't mean that you have to have a brick-and-mortar building and compete with Microsoft or Wal-Mart. I'm talking about doing something that allows you to, at first, make an income that allows you to meet your basic needs and enjoy yourself while you're doing so. Who knows, perhaps in the future you may be competing with Microsoft or Wal-Mart.

Some possible ideas might be sewing, knitting (people love custom clothes), walking pets or pet sitting, making jewelry, writing, editing, organizing closets, gardening/landscaping, cooking for busy professionals, or baking custom birthday cakes, singing or speaking.

Turn this opportunity of not having a job into a blessing. If you have no way of getting by <u>at all</u> then take a job that you can stand to go to. This is not your dream job, but it will be the job that supports you until you create your dream business or dream job.

Just because it is not your dream job and you think of it as temporary, <u>don't slack off!</u> Do the job as if you owned the company. For instance, if you work at a fast food restaurant, treat the customers as if they were your own. Don't get in the habit of doing just enough to get buy. Over-deliver.

This job is good practice for when you are in you own business or ideal job. You want to already be in the habit of giving good service and treating customers or clients well. So treat your "on the way job" with respect.

If the job really sucks, just tell yourself, "This is temporary. I'm only in training for something more wonderful and exciting that is coming my way. This job is just giving me the money I need so that I can do what I really want to do." When you are away from the job, spend time planning and working on your own business.

Of course, if the job is really degrading or painful in any way, leave immediately. Trust that you can find a job that is more pleasant, or a way of getting the money you need while planning your new business venture.

Build a Friendly Relationship with Money

"I have enough money to last me the rest of my life, unless I buy something." - Jackie Mason

I think it is safe to say that the desire for money is the pulse that drives our whole world. Motivational speaker and author Zig Ziglar said, "Money is not the most important thing in life, but it is reasonably close to oxygen." I don't think anyone can dispute that we all need money.

Have you ever felt any of these feelings about money or the lack of it? Secretive, defensive, happy, angry, free, embarrassed, frustrated, guilty, stressed or depressed. Money or the lack of it has a way of stirring up our emotions. However, it is not really the money that is causing us pain or joy; it is our perception of it, and the events associated with it.

I have met people who are being treated for depression who I felt that if someone showed them how to work through their financial stresses, they would be just fine. In fact, I've felt that way myself.

If you have a whole lot of money, it seems people feel you need to share it with them and others. They somehow feel they have the right to tell you what to do with it. "Give something back!" I hear people say. If you have very little money, people say, "Get a job. You're just lazy. Stop wasting my tax money!" Well, it appears that when it comes to money, you're "slammed if you do" and "slammed if you don't."

On one of the motivational tapes I listened to, the author said, "If you don't have the money that you desired to have, it is because you don't have the right relationship with money." I used to play that part over and over and over because I didn't 'get it'. I had never heard of having a *relationship* with money and what did that mean really?

Since that time, I now understand it. Or, perhaps I should say, I know what it means to me. To me it means feeling and interacting and thinking about money the same as I would think and feel and interact in order to build a strong, healthy and loving relationship with another person.

Let me explain. If I don't think well of someone—if I don't show someone that I am interested in them—if I tell them they are not important—if I take them for granted—if I think that they are the cause of all evil—if I don't take time to get to know them—if I feel I have to keep my relationship with them a secret because I'm afraid people will not like me if they know

I am with them—if I feel guilty for having someone in my life—if I am continuously thinking, I'm afraid they're going to leave me one day, then, surely they will. Talking and feeling negatively about people is not going to attract wonderful people into my life. They are not going to want to be around me. Would you? Well, the same goes for money.

Erase the word poor from you vocabulary. Never even joke about it. The psyche doesn't know the difference between what is real and imagined. Poor means lesser quality, as in poor workmanship. Poor means deprived unfortunate, and underprivileged. We are none of these things, never have been any of these things, and never will be any of these things.

We may be broke from time to time. Some of us may be broke for a long time. However, broke is a temporary situation—a temporary lack of money. If something is broke, it can be fixed.

Worry and frustration is not going to pay a single bill for you. Worry and frustration will interfere with you coming up with a solution that you need to move forward. Doing any of the things I've talked about in terms of diet, meditation and anything that can make you feel better is going to help relieve the stress. Once you relieve the stress, you're going to be open to receive information and ideas that will help you find solutions. Ideas will seemingly come out of the blue.

As I continue to feel better about myself, my finances don't appear so bad to me. The less stressful I am in general, the less stressed-out I am about money. One book that still brings me comfort today is a book entitled *The Game of Life and How to Play It* by Florence Scovel-Shin.

This book was published in 1925. This little inspirational book helped me understand that life is not a battle but a game of giving and receiving. This book further helped me understand the power of thoughts and words. Many times when I would be in need of a certain amount of money at a certain time, I would read sections of her book where she would be instructing someone who also needed a certain amount of money at a certain time how to relax, let go, and how to focus your mind in such a way that you open yourself up to receive.

Although I don't believe in dwelling on past events, I came up with this exercise that I find helpful. When I'm in a financial crunch, I think back and remember some of my past financial crunches. I remind myself that I didn't know how I was going to make it through those times. Yet, somehow I did. I tell myself that same power that got me through so many other challenges will also get me through this one.

Please do not feel embarrassed or ashamed if you are now, or at some point, in need of financial assistance (i.e. public assistance, food stamps, and public housing). The general public is led to believe that people who receive these types of grants are generally unworthy and lazy. While it is true there are some trifling people who are taking advantage of the system, the majority of the people on public assistance do not want to be there. There are trifling people in most organizations, corporations and governmental agencies too.

The term 'corporate welfare" was coined by Ralph Nader in 1966. There are many huge, well-known corporations that receive billions of dollars each year in the form of grants and other United States government subsidies. This is known as corporate welfare. How many times have you heard about a bank or a corporation being "bailed" out by the government? So, if you need assistance, think of it as just a bail-out. Use it, get back on your feet and move on.

Also, understand that there is nothing shameful about wanting to have beautiful and wonderful things in your life. Do you believe that you deserve an abundant life? What we attract in our lives is totally in accordance to what we believe about it, whether consciously or unconsciously.

Start learning all you can about money. The number one source that I recommend is Robert Kiyosaki. If you have not done so already read, or find a way to get a recording of his book *Rich Dad, Poor Dad*. Although this book was published in 2000, and some details may be dated now, I found his story and unique economic perspective interesting, easy to understand, and financially inspiring.

Another book that I found informative, helpful and financially inspiring for anyone dealing with debt—specifically credit card debt was Kevin Trudeau's *Debt Cures –They Don't Want You To Know About*. This book is chocked full of information and inspiration that will help you deal with any debt you may have from a more empowered position.

"Whatever is expressed is impressed. Whatever you say to yourself, with emotion, generates thoughts, ideas and behaviors consistent with those words."
    - Brian Tracy

"Water is the only drink for a wise man."
- Henry David Thoreau

You can survive many weeks without food, but only a few days without water. Dehydration will cause your body and your brain to shut down. Being happy and having a great attitude is impossible if your body is dehydrated. Drink plenty of water.

One rule is to drink half your body weight in ounces each day. That is, if you weight 200 pounds, drink 100 ounces of water. Drink filtered or spring water if possible. The tap water in many of our cities contains chemicals and, again, we cannot be sure how these chemicals are affecting us.

Juice, soda, coffee and tea are fluids. However, they are not water. F. Batmanghelidj, M.D., the author of *Your Body's Many Cries For Water* says, "The mistaken assumption that all fluids are equivalent to water for the water needs of the human body is the main cause of many of the ills of the human body, and it is frequently associated with the initial excessive gain in weight."

I remember reading that years ago prisons only had water to treat all medical problems. Like almost everything else related to health, there are contradictions, and even controversy about the water issue. There are some who still feel like John Stuart Blackie who said, "Wine is the drink of the gods, milk the drink of babes, tea the drink of women, and water the drink of beasts."

Again, I say check it out for yourself. What if you made sure you drank the above recommended amount of water every day for at least 30 days? What if you stopped drinking alcohol, soda and coffee? Hey, I'm just saying . . .

Move Your Body

We all know the body needs to move. Your brain needs a good supply of blood in order to work properly. It is the times when we feel the worst that moving our bodies could probably benefit us the most. Yet, it is at these times when exercise is the last thing we want to do—it is the last thing we re-member to do. Who wants to move when we're tired, depressed, angry or stressed?

However, if we could make a conscious effort to move when we are feeling low, we can recover and feel better much faster. Just play uplifting and happy music and dance. Sounds crazy? Don't knock it if you haven't tried it. Play music that reminds you of happy times. Stretch out those parts of your body you are able to stretch. Move, move, move. Dance, dance, dance. Your body, your mind, and your soul will thank you.

I own two pieces of exercise equipment. I own a rebounder, which is a small trampoline, and an inverter table. I secure my feet to the inverter table and it slowly rotates backward until I'm upside-down 180 degrees. I hang there for about ten minutes. Inverting uses gravity to straighten the spine. It's fun and relaxing.

I find rebounding fun as well. In my opinion, I get a good general work out from rebounding. In his book, *The Cancer Answer*, Albert Earl Carter goes into detail about how rebounding cleanses the lymphatic system and strengthens cells in our body and helps to combat osteoporosis, among other things. I love to jump up and down, and I love hanging upside down.

"If the only prayer you said in your whole life was, 'thank you,' that would suffice."
- Meister Eckhart

If ever things are not going the way you had planned. If ever you are having a challenging day. If ever you don't see a way out of a so-called bad situation. If ever you are sad about something. If ever you are feeling mad about something. If ever you just feel like giving up.

Here's the solution: Say, "Thank You."

Be still and think of all of the wonderful things you do have to be grateful for and say, "Thank you."

Are you still breathing? Be thankful for that. Can you breathe without the aid of machines? Be thankful for that. Surely there is something for you to be grateful for. Do you have two ears? Can you hear— even a little bit? Be grateful for that. Can you walk? Can you talk? Did you eat today? Does someone care about you? Do you care about somebody?

Find that something, or things that you can be thankful for and silently (or loudly, depending on where you are and who you are with) say, "Thank you Universe," or "Thank you God," or "Thank you God-in-me (or however you address the greatest infinite power) for these wonderful blessings!" Say it like you mean it.

Yes, you are counting your blessings. This is not a new idea; however, few of us realize how potent the idea is. Focus on what is right in your life. Focus on what is good in your life. Be grateful for these things.

I promise you that one or all of these five things will happen when you create an Attitude of Gratitude:

(1) The way you view the negative situation will change for the better. (2) The situation will change for the better. (3) The situation and the way you view it will change for the better. (4) Fear and anxiety will move out of your way. (5) You will experience a sense of calm that will allow you to think more clearly.

Try it. I think you'll be pleasantly surprised. Even if you are convinced you can't think of anything to be thankful for, just say the words "thank you" repeatedly for at least a couple of minutes or more, either to yourself or out loud.

Teach your young children this exercise as a game. I call it the "Gratitude Game." Let them take turns telling each other what they are thankful for. The gratitude game is a great game to play in place of a prayer or meditation before a meal. Children of all ages (this includes you) will benefit greatly from playing this game just before bedtime and/or first thing in the morning.

There is no way you can have a miserable day if you create an Attitude of Gratitude. Every day will be a great day!

" . . . Those miracles that they talk about every day. They're not miracles at all, they are the natural order of things. But because they are rare, people think they are miraculous. They're not. That's the way it is supposed to be. You're supposed to thrive."
- Abraham-Hicks

The purpose of this book is not to convince you of any particular thoughts or techniques or lifestyles but to encourage you to open your mind and take charge of your life and learn to celebrate it. What a wonderful goal! Getting healthy and happy so you can seize life and love it.

You are in the exact, perfect, right place to begin again. If you have a dream, go for it. If you don't have a dream or a fabulous goal, get one. You know one reason that most people don't go after their dreams? They are afraid that if they try something different, people might say "YOU'RE Crazy." We already know we're crazy. So what is to stop us from dreaming big and going for it—and succeeding!

The Beginning!

About the Author

Wambui Bahati is an actress, singer, writer, storyteller, inspirational and motivational speaker. She began her formal theatrical studies at New York University School of the Arts and made her professional theatrical debut in *Godspell* at Ford's Theater in Washington, D.C. She went on to perform in the Broadway productions of *Godspell* and *Jesus Christ Superstar.*

Wambui's regional and touring credits include starring roles in *The Magic Show,* Joseph Papp's rock version of *Two Gentlemen of Verona, Little Ham, Nunsense, Don't Bother Me, I Can't Cope, Gone With the Wind*—the musical, *The Wiz* and *Crowns.*

Wambui wrote, produced, and stars in the one-woman musicals *Balancing Act* and *I Am Domestic Violence.* Both of these shows have received national acclaim for the unique way that they provide outstanding entertainment while dealing with important issues in our communities.

Ms. Bahati possesses the uncanny ability to create custom shows and presentations based on a specific theme or topic. She has written and performed these custom presentations for organizations such as NOW (National Organization for Women), Habitat for Humanity, and the Carter Center.

Some of her awards include a Woman of Achievement Award from the Greensboro Commission on the Status of Women, a Belle Ringer Image Award from Bennett College, the Lionel Aldridge Award (a national honor recognizing individuals who provide extraordinary service and courage on behalf of people with mental illnesses), the National Alliance for the Mentally Ill, North Carolina's President's Award, and a proclamation from the mayor of the city of Toledo, Ohio.

Named John Ann Washington at birth, Wambui Bahati is her new legal name taken on during the "reinvention of herself." In Swahili, Wambui means "singer of songs," Bahati means, "my fortune is good." The native North Carolinian lives in New York City and is the proud mother of two adult daughters.

Her passion: "Reminding You of Your Magnificence."

www.wambui.com

We hope you enjoyed this
JLW World Press Book

WAMBUI WOULD LOVE TO HEAR FROM YOU

We invite you to leave an audio comment
or testimonial about this book.
You may do so by calling: (214) 615-6044 ext **1508**

Please visit our website
www.you-dont-know-crazy.com
and join our mailing list to find out when the *You Don't
Know Crazy* book signing tour is coming to a city near
you. You can also join our 'snail' mail list by sending
your name and address to
JLW World Press

BOOK WAMBUI FOR YOUR NEXT EVENT!
Contact Mark Steiner at marks@steinertalent.com
866-319-0050
or
www.you-dont-know-crazy.com
888-224-2267

For information about special discounts for
bulk purchases, please contact
JLW World Press
244 Fifth Avenue, Suite 2048
New York, NY 10001
212-537-0441

Breinigsville, PA USA
25 September 2010
246056BV00001B/80/P